Women and the Military

Women and the Military

Over 100 Notable Contributors, Historic to Contemporary

by JOHN P. DEVER
and MARIA C. DEVER

with a foreword by
BRIGADIER GENERAL EVELYN P. FOOTE

McFarland & Company, Inc., Publishers
Jefferson, North Carolina, and London

British Library Cataloguing-in-Publication data are available

Library of Congress Cataloguing-in-Publication Data

Dever, John Patrick.
   Women and the military : over 100 notable contributors, historic
to contemporary / by John P. Dever and Maria Dever ; with a foreword
by Evelyn P. Foote.
     p. cm.
   Includes bibliographical references (p.) and index.
   ISBN 0-89950-976-2 (lib. bdg. : 55# alk. paper) ∞
   1. Women soldiers—Biography. 2. Women and the military.
I. Dever, Maria. II. Title.
UB416.D48 1995
355.2'2'082—dc20
[B]
                                                   94-30910
                                                     CIP

Manufactured in the United States of America

McFarland & Company, Inc., Publishers
  Box 611, Jefferson, North Carolina 28640

Dedicated to all who fight the good fight

Acknowledgments ———————————

Our research was done at the United States Military Academy at West Point, New York. Also, as a staff and faculty member of the Second United States Army Area Intelligence School (SUSAAIS) at Fort Bragg, North Carolina, for over a decade, John had access to several libraries at Fort Bragg which included the John F. Kennedy Warfare School library and the archives of the 82nd Airborne Division. Further, he interviewed several active duty women, including Cheryl Stearns, the first woman member of the Golden Knights, the 82nd's internationally known parachute organization.

Ellen P. Murdock, chairperson of the Defense Advisory Committee on Women in the Services, Washington, D.C., was very encouraging to us throughout, as was Peggy Heusinkveld, Media Publications Manager for Women in the Military, a non-profit foundation located in the U.S. capital. Our list of individuals and organizations that assisted us could be much longer, but we are particularly indebted to those aforementioned.

Contents —————————————

Contents

Preface

The history of women in the military is replete with injustice and inexplicable contradiction. But it is also full of brilliant chapters revealing the determination of brave soldiers who want to command, above all, respect. Using the United States as an example one can see the sacrifices women have made, all the while realizing that their deeds would receive little recognition.

The Civil War nurses were patriotic, dedicated women who provided extraordinary examples of devotion, sacrifice, preparation, courage, and endurance. There was extreme opposition, simply because of their sex, to bestowing military status upon them. Intelligence and skill did not matter; gender did.

During the Vietnam War, the 7th Air Force, Pacific Air Force (PACAF) sent an urgent communique to the personnel center to cancel all future WAF assignments to units of the 7th Air Force because of the harsh combat conditions. The WAF presently assigned to the 7th were to be replaced by men. However, there is no indication that the 7th Air Force was preparing to evacuate its civilian employees. Jeanne M. Holm, WAF director, justifiably insisted that if a decision were made to send all U.S. women out of the area, the WAF should be the last to leave. The military women overwhelmingly agreed. The performance of military women during the Vietnam War should have proven irrevocably to all that women are effective in a combat environment. It didn't.

When the United States invaded Panama, Kim Schmidz, then in the active army, helped to secure an airport while being showered by enemy fire. Had this been an "official" war, she, as a woman, would have suddenly been unsuitable for the job. During the Persian Gulf War, women loaded bombs onto jet fighter planes, piloted helicopters into Iraqi airspace, and were killed by Scud missiles. Over 35,000 women served admirably in this war. Yet the Pentagon maintains that women will not perform well under the stress of battle.

There continues to be, even as we near the end of the twentieth century, a campaign to limit opportunities for women in the U.S. military, with the Marine Corps emerging as the most restrictive of the services in utilizing women. Many men and even some women want to prove that women are physically and mentally weaker than men and therefore not as effective in the country's fighting force despite proof to the contrary. Nervously they are gathering ammunition to protect the aura of maleness traditionally associated with the military.

Throughout the 1980s the Department of Defense, with increasing desperation, attempted to reaffirm so-called traditional values, in order to justify their exclusionary policies. Research studies were conducted to determine the level at which women decrease the combat readiness of a unit. The results of these studies repeatedly indicated that women performed well with the unit and that the key to a unit's performance is not based on the male to female ratio, but rather on the unit's leadership. Such studies are reminiscent of the scientist who conducts an experiment to prove his hypothesis and at the experiment's end, confirms the hypothesis in spite of the results because he simply knows he cannot be wrong.

But what the Defense Department forgot was that they were speaking to a new generation of Americans who had grown up exposed to the ugly wound of prejudice. They had learned to mistrust so-called research studies, graphs and grids telling them what and how to think. U.S. Representative Pat Schroeder (D–Colorado) voiced some of their concerns when the Commission on the Assignment of Women in the Armed Forces was established by Congress in 1991 to examine the laws and policies restricting the assignments of women service members. Schroeder was very critical of President George Bush's fifteen appointees to the commission, insisting, "Women in the military will never get a fair shake because this commission is chock-full of old school military thinkers. When the commission report comes back opposing further gains for servicewomen, all I will have to say is: Consider the source." Though women have been afforded more opportunities in recent years, they are still locked out of many jobs, resulting in fewer promotions to the higher ranks. At this moment, women are not allowed to fly special operations aircraft nor can they serve in field artillery units that employ the Multiple Launch Rocket System (MLRS). By excluding women from MLRS, the Army's three combat arms branches — infantry, armor and field artillery — remain an all-male bastion.

It is difficult to envision today an army without women. Yet the message to military women remains the same: If there is a conflict, they had better be there and when it is all over, they are expected to keep on the camouflage and remain invisible. There is no question that the attitudes still present in society have hurt women. Work done by women has historically been perceived as less important than work done by men. Incredibly, it was not until the *Frontiero v. Richardson* (1973) ruling that dependents of military women were given the same entitlements as those given to the dependents of military men.

There are those who believe that the United States will be perceived as weak if women are defending it. Yet all over the world, from the Russians to Central Americans to the Israelis, women have been allowed into combat. Yet the whole notion of "allowing" women into combat is disturbing. "Allowing" women to do or not to do something is a remnant of the paternalistic society. A grown woman should go as far as talent and hard work allow her to go. By excluding women from key positions in the Armed Forces, we deny both the women the chance to further their careers in the service and, perversely, deny the military the skilled and qualified people available to help complete its mission — defending the country.

If at the beginning of this century a little girl had said that she wanted to become a general or a commander, all would have laughed at her. The last two generations, though, have witnessed many "firsts" for women, among them the signing by President Lyndon Johnson in 1967 of a law which gave more career opportunities to women and the opening of the Reserve Officer Training Corps (ROTC) to females. Just as co-education has brought about the acceptance of women as equals among students, so it was hoped that the young men in the military academies would perceive women as professionals like themselves when they opened their doors to women in 1976. But the acceptance of women has been extremely slow, with significant incidents of sexual harassment. Women will not be entirely accepted by their male counterparts until they are "allowed" into combat and put their lives on the line for their country as every male soldier must.

Foreword

Women are an integral part of American military history. From the American Revolution through Desert Storm, courageous women have stepped forward to help build, protect and defend the United States. Yet, recognition of women's military roles and, in fact, the right of women to serve in our armed forces are, in the main, happenings of the twentieth century.

This book is about brave, patriotic women — all volunteers — who have stepped forward to be counted and to serve their countries in times of peace and war. Some of them had to masquerade as men in order to enlist — those who fought in our battles prior to World War I. And, in that "Great War to end all wars," only a few thousand women were permitted to enlist in the United States Navy and the Marine Corps. Women also served as Navy or Army nurses but were not given rank or benefits equal to those provided male officers.

Some of the biographies you read will be about women who were never given military status or recognition. Some served as civilians in support of our national defense effort. All of the women portrayed, however, are pioneers in service who have helped advance military career opportunities for women.

In my three decades of military service, I met a number of the women whose stories appear in this book. Some of these great pioneers, such as Oveta Culp Hobby of the Army, Mildred McAfee of the Navy, Ruth C. Streeter of the Marines, and Dorothy C. Stratton of the Coast Guard, led the way for all of us in forming and leading the women's corps of their services in World War II. Also featured are biographies of some of their successors — outstanding women of the 1990s, such as Major Marie T. Rossi, an Army pilot who died when her helicopter crashed in Saudi Arabia, and Captain

Linda Bray, U.S. Army, credited as the first woman to lead American troops in battle during Operation Just Cause in Panama.

The stories told here are but a fraction of the history and heritage of America's women in uniform. On sea, on land and in the air, women in the armed forces, filling thousands of vital military roles, continue to serve their country in times of both peace and war. I am truly proud to be a part of that heritage and history.

EVELYN P. FOOTE
Brigadier General
United States Army (Retired)

Introduction ————————————————————

A fair scrutiny of history shows that women have participated as soldiers, guerrillas or paramilitary forces in armed conflicts throughout the world. More recently their roles have increased dramatically. Women serve on aircraft carriers, fly transport and refueling aircraft, drive trucks transporting men and matériel; they work as technicians, mechanics, interrogators, and perform medical and guard duties.

The common denominator of all who serve in the military is courage and a willingness to do one's duty. Incredibly, there are those who feel that women's participation in the military somehow threatens a country's national security. Nothing could be further from the truth. It is our hope to illustrate through these biographies the fallacy of this notion and draw attention to the bravery and selflessness of women in combat since the beginning of recorded time. We therefore have included women to represent all ages, from the pre–Christian era to today. Since women's contributions also transcend culture and country, we have included exemplary women from such diverse origins as Egypt, Hungary, Lithuania, Zimbabwe, Greece, the former Soviet Union, China, Ireland, Britain, the Philippines, France, Rhodes, and the United States of America.

Although any woman who undertakes the defense of her homeland and beliefs deserves to be honored, it would not have been possible to include all of them in this book. Therefore the inclusion criteria are based on whether (1) the woman was a "first" at something, a pioneer whose trail-blazing opened the way for other women; (2) the woman had an unusual or extraordinary experience in the military, requiring her ingenuity as well as her bravery; (3) the woman had led an exemplary life, to which anyone, soldier or otherwise, should aspire; or (4) the woman had endured extraordinary prejudice.

To begin our research, we defined the military as a group of people united for the purpose of national defense. This group includes unrecognized women who defended their homeland or beliefs through combat, intelligence operations, or a support role.

Because of discrepancies in the amount of research material we were able to obtain, some of the biographies are shorter than others. This should not be taken as an indication of relative importance.

*When a just cause reaches its flood tide . . .
whatever stands in the way must fall before its
overwhelming power.*

CARRIE CHAPMAN CATT

Major
Biographies

Clara Barton

A hundred years ago life was very different for women all over the world, and the United States was no exception. Many years had to pass before women were given the vote, and women had virtually no access to the professions. There were few colleges for women, and it was unthinkable to have a woman in a position of authority over men. The role of women varied widely with their social class, but they were all expected to be pious, raise their children, work in the house, and be supportive of their husbands to whom they deferred all important decisions. Of course women needed to learn to read for how else could they read the Bible? And they needed to be able to keep the household accounts. In this social status of upper class families, young girls were accomplished in womanly pursuits: music, painting, art, history, and polite salon conversation. A young girl should be able to dance prettily and write a letter in a well-formed, stylish handwriting. Women blessed with a fortune and a position in society visited the poor, and spent their evenings embroidering dainty slippers or chair covers. But a girl most decidedly did not discuss politics or meddle in men's affairs for which, both men and many women thought, she was not suited by nature.

Yet the time when Clara Barton lived was interesting. Politically, America was readying for change. Slavery was an issue even if the Civil War was still years away. Authors like Nathaniel Hawthorne, Ralph Waldo Emerson, Edgar Allan Poe, and others were writing. In rural America life was still very hard. People ate what they grew and clothing was made by the women of the family. Work lasted from sun-up to sundown. Many farms were isolated, and most neighbors saw each other at Sunday church services unless a blizzard made the unpaved roads impassable.

On Christmas Day, 1821, Clara was born to the Bartons in North Oxford, Massachusetts, a family already consisting of two daughters and two sons, much too old to be playmates for the new baby girl. The father, a well-to-do farm owner, had been an Indian fighter in western lands. Barton hung on her father's every word as he told her of his adventures in the exciting and, to Barton, faraway frontier. But Barton's father was not merely an adventurer; he had served in the Massachusetts legislature and been a selectman in his own town. Her mother, though kind, did not believe in pampering children and was strict with the little girl. She was not given toys to play with, but at the age when most girls nowadays are entering kindergarten Barton could ride a pony. The discipline she was taught at home served her in good stead throughout her life. Perhaps because she grew up in an accomplished household comprised of almost grown-up siblings, Barton was reading by age three. She thirsted for knowledge and books were her friends. It is no wonder that as an adult Barton turned to teaching.

When the time came, Barton was well-prepared to take charge of the one-room schoolhouse and the pupils of all ages that she was assigned. Though she excelled at her job, after a few years Barton decided that she needed a change. In search of new horizons, she traveled to the Liberal Institute at Clinton, New York, to pursue her education. The Liberal Institute was one of the very few institutions where women teachers could continue their learning. It was strictly a female establishment; in those days co-educational institutions of higher learning did not exist.

The Institute was a wonderful place for Barton and her happiness is reflected in her diary entries. Yet there were also moments of deep pain, such as the death of her mother. Her suffering during this time leaps from the page and touches the heart of those who read her diaries.

During a visit to a friend in Bordentown, New Jersey, in 1852, Barton observed many children idly roaming the streets. Why weren't they in school? Well, there were no schools in the community that were free, and those that were available for pay were reserved to those more deserving of the privilege. After all, these children were nothing but street urchins. Barton's indignation took the form of action.

Using what influence she possessed, Barton was able to appropriate an old schoolhouse for her plans of teaching these same street children. The prediction of the town was that the young lady would tire of her project and dedicate herself to more worthy causes. On the first day of school six children appeared at the door; a year later six hundred children were being taught by Barton herself or by some of the friends she recruited. So impressed was the Board of Education and the whole town that in 1853 a new schoolhouse was built to accommodate the children. Clara Barton should have been the principal, but it was unthinkable to give a woman such authority. Tragically the job was given to a young man who, mediocre himself and jealous of Barton's success, made his authority felt every moment. Her life became so miserable that she resigned. But jobs for women were limited to teaching school or becoming a governess, or if a girl had no education, she could become a servant and be trained in a household. Pay for any of these jobs was minimal, and there were no retirement or insurance to cover illness or old age.

Because her qualifications were excellent and she was highly recommended, Barton became a copy clerk in the Patent Office in Washington, a very difficult job in those days before typewriters. Soon Barton was earning $1400 a year, a very considerable sum, particularly for a woman. Judge Charles Mason, her boss, made her his confidential clerk in an attempt to stop the leaks and corruption which were rampant in his office. But by 1856 the Democrats were in power in Washington and Judge Mason and Barton were asked to resign. Frustrated by men who perceived women as threats and who thought women incapable of performing jobs the men did, in some cases, so badly themselves, Barton returned to her ailing father. However, she had done such an outstanding job that she was soon recalled to her former position despite the partisan leaning of the Patent Office.

Times were troubled in the young United States. Hand-to-hand combats often followed the bitter harangues of the abolitionists. Southern states threatened to secede from the Union. On February 18, 1861, President Jefferson Davis assumed the presidency of the new Confederacy. The beginning of the Civil War was the impulse that Clara Barton needed to swing into action. With her clear thinking, she perceived the danger of transporting the wounded soldiers and treating them far from the field of battle, a common practice in that era. Instead, argued Miss Barton, let them be tended and consoled as near as possible to where they suffered the wounds. In this way many needless deaths would be avoided, and those dying would receive consolation. Women, thought Barton, were by nature better nurses than men; allow them, then, to participate in the nursing. Had not Florence Nightingale proven to the whole world women's value as nurses? Most men, and indeed, most women were not ready to alter their ideas on this subject: women belonged in the home and not in public life.

In 1862, the U.S. Army Surgeon General William Hammond finally gave his permission for Clara Barton to nurse and comfort the sick and wounded — but always under the authority of the doctors, whose orders she must obey implicitly. Despite all the restrictions, Barton was elated and in August she left for the battlefield.

Barton was present at Culpeper, Virginia, to nurse and comfort the men, all the while writing frantic letters to keep the supplies coming. When casualties from the second battle of Bull Run were laid on bales of hay, Barton and her three volunteers tended to them. On September 13, 1862, Barton learned that the supplies she was carrying to Harpers Ferry were of vital importance, and she pushed on through the night to assist the wounded by daybreak. Her work was so extraordinary that Abraham Lincoln asked Barton to review the troops with him, an honor indeed.

The winter of 1862 announced its arrival with some of the coldest weather. Snow, sleet and freezing rain fell for days and Barton, constantly exposed to the elements as she nursed the sick and tended to the dying, developed a severe inflammation in one hand. When she attempted to return to Washington for treatment, she was summoned back to the front. The battle of Fredericksburg was brutal. With tears in her eyes from the pain of her swollen hand, Barton worked feverishly. The cold was cruel and froze the wounded to the ground. Through day and through night Barton and her volunteers labored. She made sure that hot soup was available for those with sufficient energy to drink it.

By the spring of 1863, Barton felt she could leave the Army of the Potomac. She knew that a battle would occur near Hilton Head, an island off South Carolina, and she meant to be there for her assistance would be needed. After the failure of the seige of Charleston, Barton was certain that she could not keep going. An illness forced her to retreat to the North. How could she afford ill health when so many wounded soldiers lay suffering on the fields of the nation? Despite such misgivings she realized that she must retire from active life for a while.

In her brief retirement, she found there was something else she could do. She dispatched letters reaching to government officials, philanthropists, and civic organizations, for there was no organized welfare program, only voluntary contributions.

As soon as she felt a little stronger, Barton went back to the front, this time to the Wilderness campaign in the thick woods near the Rapidan River. Here she faced a great disaster — a brush fire, impossible to control, burned many of the wounded. Later, non-stop rains churned the earth into mud; wagons got stuck and the wounded could not be moved. Barton knew most would die if nothing was done.

Collecting four fast horses, she rode nonstop to the dock. There she boarded a steamer for Washington where she met with Senator Henry Wilson, then chairman of the Senate military committee. Clara Barton concisely related to him the condition of the wounded and implored him to help. She was so convincing and so earnest that early the next morning the quartermaster general and his staff rushed help to the battlefield. Barton spent two days getting supplies ready, and by the third day she was back on the scene of action.

In June of 1864 Clara Barton was appointed superintendent of the Department of Nurses for the Army of the James under General Benjamin Butler. The general relied on her judgment and allowed her to proceed without having to wait for orders, an honor never before conferred on a woman, more significant since women's powers of reasoning were not considered to be on a par with men's.

Southerners now believed that the North would win the war.

Its armies outnumbered those of the Confederacy and its supplies and war matériel were ample, whereas the resources of the South, in men, food, and equipment, were exhausted. Indeed, General Robert E. Lee surrendered to General U.S. Grant at Appomattox, Virginia, and the war was over. While it lasted, Barton had proved to Americans and to other nations across the globe that women could succeed in work previously done only by men.

By 1869 Barton was again on the move, this time abroad. She enjoyed her tour of European cities but, acknowledging that she needed a rest, she decided to stop a few months in Geneva and temporarily break away from her many chores. She should have known better. Preceded by the name she had made for herself, she was sought out by a Swiss delegation who wished an explanation of why the United States had failed to ratify the Geneva Convention. Barton had no answer; in fact, she knew nothing about it. But she was impressed by the noble aims of the organization and determined to work for its cause.

In Europe, as in America, Barton worked to improve the lot of others who were willing to help themselves. To this end she used her own money to set up a clothes factory where poor women could make garments later sold for profit; thus the women were no longer objects of charity, rather they could take pride in their accomplishments while taking home a sizeable income. What difference did it make that they first started sewing in the yard of a ruined and abandoned house? They had material and patterns, and their work accomplished the rest. After she saw that the operation was running smoothly and bringing a handsome profit to the workers, Barton did not linger.

Back in the United States, Clara Barton was elected president of the Association of the American Red Cross. Soon thereafter the association was put to the test. A fire broke out in Michigan, burning out of control and consuming half the state. Barton and her volunteers packed box upon box of food and clothing, proving the efficiency of the association by meeting a national emergency and providing invaluable help within hours of the onset of the emergency.

Other women across the Atlantic were battling for their rights. A new era dawned for women everywhere, and Clara Barton proudly accepted an offer to represent the United States at the International Conference of the Red Cross in Geneva. She had come a long way from those days in Bordentown, New Jersey. By now the Red Cross was known, respected, and supported by people all over the United States. Barton herself received many honors from regiments and from kings, from presidents at home and from such diverse people as Otto von Bismarck and Leo Tolstoi abroad.

There were few times when Clara Barton had not lent her help and support. When the dam near Johnstown, Pennsylvania, broke in 1889, 5,000 people drowned and almost as many needed succor, and she was there. When the Armenians were starving and helpless in 1895 and 1896, Clara Barton and the American Red Cross were on the scene. If the government supported a cause, Clara Barton was there. If there was no official support, then Clara and her co-workers raised money from private sources to alleviate suffering. In 1898 Clara Barton was in Cuba caring for victims of the Spanish American War. There she met Colonel Theodore Roosevelt, later president of the United States, and there she stayed when all other U.S. citizens were evacuated to the mainland.

As the years mounted, Clara knew that she should pass the control of her beloved Red Cross to others younger than herself, but she found it very difficult to do so. As she grew older she became more rigid and somewhat suspicious as she argued with herself whether there was anyone truly as willing to dedicate herself to the Red Cross and serve it as she had. She was unable to cooperate with the new board of the Red Cross. She argued unimportant points endlessly and resented having her authority questioned; to avoid this she used her not small influence to be appointed president of the American Red Cross for life. She was affronted when Congress instituted an investigation into the Red Cross. As Barton predicted, no evidence of mismanagement was found and the investigation was dropped. However, Barton's judgment now lacked the sharpness that had been one of her most valuable characteristics.

Finally, her good sense asserted itself and on May 14, 1904,

Clara Barton resigned from the Red Cross. Her path had been arduous, her honors many. Looking back upon her life, Barton saw long years of service and sacrifice. She could have married— certainly she had enough offers—but she knew that what she wanted from life was not compatible with marriage. By her actions she had advanced the status of women, and she herself never ceased to grow spiritually and intellectually. On April 12, 1912, at age 91, Clara Barton died.

Florence Blanchfield

Colonel Florence Blanchfield once described her military career as similar to the itinerary of a traveling salesman. A veritable ball of energy, she had been all over the world, serving in both World War I and World War II.

Born on April 1, 1884, Blanchfield first attended business college in Pittsburgh, then took classes at the University of California and Columbia University. She found her true vocation in nursing, and graduated from the South Side Training School for Nurses in Pittsburgh. She then sought further instruction in surgical technique and operating room supervision at Johns Hopkins Hospital. For the next several years, Blanchfield held a variety of posts: supervisor of the operating room of Pittsburgh's South Side and Montefiore hospitals; superintendent of the Suburban General Hospital in Bellevue, Pennsylvania; general duty nurse and anesthetist at the Canal Zone Hospital in Panama in 1913; and industrial nurse at the U.S. steel plant in Bessemer, Pennsylvania.

In 1917, when the United States decided to enter World War I, Blanchfield joined the Army Nurse Corps which was the start of her illustrious career in the Army. From September 27, 1917 to May 13, 1919, she was on active duty in France. After that she served in military hospitals in Michigan and Indiana. She soon became a teacher and recreational director at the Army School of Nursing at Letterman General Hospital in California, and later went overseas to serve in the Philippines.

In 1925 Blanchfield returned to the United States, working at Walter Reed General Hospital in Washington, D.C., and as special duty nurse at the home of the secretary of war. Blanchfield then resumed her traveling career, holding a succession of positions in Georgia, Missouri, the Philippines, China, and California. In 1935 she started work in the office of the surgeon general.

In March 1942, after the outbreak of World War II, Blanchfield was commissioned as a lieutenant colonel in the U.S. Army. She served as first assistant to Colonel Julia Flikke, superintendent of the Army Nurse Corps. Although Blanchfield and Flikke both held high rank, they did not receive appropriate pay or benefits. They held relative rank, which consists solely of a formal title, as opposed to full rank, which encompasses the title as well as the corresponding pay and benefits. As it was, Flikke was paid as a lieutenant colonel and Blanchfield was paid as a major.

When illness forced Colonel Flikke to retire, Blanchfield ascended on June 1, 1943, to the post of superintendent of the Army Nurse Corps. Surgeon General Norman T. Kirk pinned on the silver eagles that signified her promotion to colonel. At that time, only one other woman in the U.S. Army held a colonel's position, and that was Oveta Culp Hobby, director of the Women's Army Corps (WAC).

In her new position, Blanchfield oversaw 60,000 nurses in the United States and overseas. She diligently read, often far into the night, reports which the nurses sent so that she could better supervise and assist them in their mission.

Blanchfield also fought to obtain full military rank for nurses in the Army. By April 1947 both the Army and Navy changed their policy and allowed women to hold full rank. In that same year, General Dwight D. Eisenhower bestowed upon Colonel Blanchfield the first regular Army commission to be held by a woman. Through Blanchfield's endeavors, the place of women in the Army was thus vastly improved. Women began to receive the stability, prestige and benefits they so richly deserved.

Colonel Blanchfield retired from the Army in 1947 at the age of 63. She lived in Arlington, Virginia, near the political and military arena, and died in Washington, D.C. on May 12, 1971.

When we think back on the era in which Florence Blanchfield lived we realize that it could not have been easy for a woman to travel as she did from Missouri to Manila, from China to Georgia. Yet one of Colonel Blanchfield's most important battles was fought at home: winning full rank for nurses instead of the relative rank which had been pinned on them by the male military establishment. By diminishing the women's importance, they underscored their own, thereby perpetuating the myth that the military is inherently a man's domain.

Boudicca *or* Boadicea

By the River Thames in London stands the statue of a majestic queen. Upright on her chariot, she warns the enemies of England that she is ready to fight for the land of her daughters. Through the ages she has been called Boadicea, Bunduica, and Boudicca. No matter, for she was the famous Queen of the Iceni, called the "powerful tribe" by Tacitus, and fearlessly she commanded the uprising of the tribes against the power of Rome 60 years into the Christian era.

This queen of history made magical by legend wore skins to cover herself rather than the silks she is portrayed as donning. She carried a sword and an axe, and she handled a bow and arrow with consummate dexterity.

Unquestionably, prejudice makes us suspicious of women in power. In some cases women are revered as was the case with Isabella of Spain and Elizabeth I of England, but this notwithstanding, we observe their military and political prowess with uneasiness. A queen must rule her country and lead the army, albeit often from afar. This role, considered proper for males, is supposedly alien to females since they are born to promote peace and healing, not to spill the blood of their people.

In that long lost age when England was covered with forests where boars ran free and the song of the Druids was heard, lived the tribe of the Iceni. An ally of Rome, they peacefully inhabited present-day Norfolk and part of Suffolk. A young girl of the tribe, Boudicca, was married to the leader, Prasutagus, and upon his death in A.D. 59 Boudicca became queen. It is hard to separate fact from fiction regarding Boudicca for there are only some references about her from Roman writers, all postdating the revolt of the tribes. It is known, however, that the Iceni people were courageous, that they were strong and farmed their land well. They loved to fight and enjoyed music and dancing. They went into battle naked, sounding their horns and trumpets, and they celebrated their victories with drink. Their well-developed bodies adorned with gold bracelets and necklaces, the Iceni were an imposing sight. Their clothing was gaily colored and they rode carts made of the wood from their forests and drawn by well-cared-for horses.

The Iceni lived in round houses with sloping roofs, a must in a country with large amounts of rainfall. A fire in the middle of their dwellings was used for both cooking and warmth during the bitterly cold winter months. If, as tradition says, there was a palace where Boudicca lived, it has not been found.

Women enjoyed a high status among the Iceni, and, as is known, were priestesses in the Druid religion. The human soul, the Iceni believed, resided in the head, and so they kept the heads of their enemies, embalming and displaying them. This practice was abhorrent to the Romans. At the time of the Iceni uprising against Rome, Boudicca, the widow of the ruler of the tribe, had two young daughters. Boudicca was tall and attractive, with an abundance of long red hair and, according to accounts, a strong voice. It is unclear what provoked the ire of the Romans toward the tribe of the Iceni, but showing a decided lack of strategy and caution for which the Romans are famous, the estate of King Prasutagus was confiscated upon his death. Some members of the court, allies and friends of the Romans found their own estates threatened and themselves humiliated. Had the Romans attempted to wreak vengeance for a clearly stated crime, the punishment could be understood, but no account has been found to this effect. Perhaps, and again uncharacteristically, the Romans seized the opportunity afforded to them by the death of an allied king to confiscate property.

Once set to demonstrate their superiority and how little they feared the Iceni, or perhaps intent on making an example for other less peaceful tribes, the Romans flogged Queen Boudicca publicly and raped her daughters. This clearly told the Iceni and others that the Romans thought themselves all-powerful and would do as they pleased.

That the Romans expected no retaliation from the Iceni now that the tribe was ruled by a woman seems obvious. To the Romans, women were weak, lacked self-control, and needed the strong discipline of a man. But the Romans had misread the situation and miscalculated the power that a woman could exert among the Britons. Queen Boudicca could, and did, exert this power on her people. Other tribes must have been very near breaking point because they too joined Boudicca, not to preserve justice for the Iceni, but rather because they had much to lose themselves.

The official motive for the war was the money given to some Iceni by the Romans who now claimed that money as a debt. There are documented accounts of excessive taxation by the Romans. But another and perhaps more grievous mistake was the Roman attempts to suppress Druidism and implant their own diametrically opposite form of worship.

The timing chosen for the uprising was excellent. Suetonius, a very able Roman leader, had taken his troops to the western edge of his territory. The gods smiled upon the venture for when Boudicca addressed her people and released a hare it ran in the right direction. The sign given by this animal, held sacred by the Britons, could not be ignored by those who might have advocated caution. With about 120,000 fighters and invoking Andreaste, the goddess of victory, Boudicca attacked Camulodunum without warning and found it completely unprepared. The warriors were aided by a force from within that was also dissatisfied with Roman rule. The peril represented by an unrestful population mingling in their midst had evidently not occurred to the Romans, perhaps because of the natural feeling of superiority of the conqueror and the certainty of the Romans that they had completely subjugated the Britons. In any case, defense was almost nil. Reinforcements from London were not quickly dispatched for the Romans thought the situation not grave. However, the Boudiccan forces and their blazes destroyed the town. The soldiers defended the temple desperately for two days and then succumbed to the rebels. They knew their fate and indeed all were killed as were their families. When the news of the massacre reached London, the pain of the loss of lives was exacerbated by the humiliation of having been defeated by a woman.

Finally realizing what the true state of affairs was, part of the IX Legion Hispana was dispatched for Camulodunum. Just north of this town the tribes set up an ambush and decimated the rescuing forces. In view of this new defeat, Governor Suetonius hastened to London and was able to beat the rebels to the city. No doubt the rebel forces were aided by the element of surprise for they were no match for the highly trained and well equipped soldiers of Rome, though they did outnumber them.

Had the Britons ambushed Suetonius on the way to London, or had they not allowed him time to prepare, they may have won and changed the course of history, since Londinium was not a fortified town, but a city spreading wide over 30 acres with more than 25,000 people. Suetonius, always a good strategist, did not even try to defend London. The citizens who could ran from the city, barely ahead of Boudicca's forces. Many others, old, young, or optimists, refused to believe the possibility of an imminent attack. All perished and their beautiful homes were destroyed. Evidence of the fires is the "red layer" of about six inches in depth and lying about fourteen feet below ground which archeologists have excavated. Boudicca did not take prisoners, a custom of the time as they brought a handsome price in the slave market. All caught were sacrificed to the goddess Andraste by the thankful tribes in the hope that the goddess would continue to smile upon them.

It is difficult to ascertain whether Boudicca herself, shrouded in the mists of time and legend, was part of the massacre or if she tried to stop it with a vision to the future. It must have been clear to her that she could not be permanently victorious against mighty Rome.

Boudicca's next target was Veralamium, another undefended

city. Most of what happened is gleaned from the evidence offered by excavations. These once again reveal a "red layer," all that is left of the burned city. Many were able to escape before Boudicca's armies swooped down upon the city, but the town itself was sacked, burned, and all those unfortunates still within its confines were killed without mercy. Loot was plentiful. This focus on ransacking may well have diverted Boudicca from the vital necessity of eradicating Suetonius's army, or at least weakening it, before he could prepare a massive counterattack. At this point the Romans could have been defeated by the rebels.

Now prepared, Suetonius attacked. He was so greatly outnumbered that by taking the initiative he could at least choose the site and moment of the battle. He chose a ravine with forests at its back; its exact location is a mystery. Accounts tell that many women fought in the armies of the Britons, possibly hurting their cause for they were even less trained for battle than the men. The men, long on courage, were short on experience and training for mostly they were farmers possessing no armor. Considering this another easy victory, the tribes brought their families to watch the engagement from their carts and cheer the combatants on, and thus neatly blocked off all possibility of retreat. The Romans, though outnumbered, were much less vulnerable, with their helmets, body armor, shields and hobnailed sandals. They had javelins that they could throw, and they carried swords and daggers. The Roman infantry moved into the enemy in wedge formation, inflicting heavy losses with the first thrust. The cavalry followed and the damage was so heavy that the Britons were sent into flight. But, alas, their wagons trapped them. Men, women, children and animals were killed.

Queen Boudicca herself outlived the battle, but her life was at an end. If we are to believe Tacitus, she took poison. No one knows whether her daughters were hidden from the Romans and survived. Perhaps Boudicca gave her daughters the same draught that she herself drank, for death would have been preferable to leaving them to the Romans. Although the superstitious conquerors allowed their enemies to bury their own dead — hoping to avoid evil spirits — there is no record of where Boudicca is buried.

Ravaged by war, their fields not planted, and their harvests not collected, a famine beset the Iceni. Other Britons continued the fight against Rome, for they knew that if in Roman hands, either by capture or surrender, no mercy could be expected. The Roman repression was cruel and directed mainly against the first to revolt. The Iceni, already deprived of their ruler, were hopeless, expent and utterly incapable of further revolt. They had tasted victory, and defeat was the more bitter for it.

Boudicca knew little of military strategy and tactics; for this she paid with her life and possibly those of her daughters, certainly with thousands of others. But the memory of her courage lives on, as she rises from the shadows of the dim past whenever a symbol of freedom is needed by other generations of Britons either on British soil or abroad. To this day she continues to spur the descendants of those early Britons onward to victory.

Sherian Grace Cadoria

Brigadier General Sherian Grace Cadoria, the first black woman general, claims that she did not find military discipline difficult because her mother was as strict as any sergeant major. One time when Cadoria and her brother and sister had walked five miles to shop in town, one of the salesclerks gave them an extra penny by mistake. When they came home with the extra penny, their mother made all three walk back to town to return it, since at least one of the three should have known better. As Cadoria herself says, that type of lesson is forever imprinted in the mind of a child.

As a girl Cadoria walked five miles to school and five miles back. The school bus passed right in front of her house but it did not stop for black children. Nevertheless Cadoria pursued her education with determination and enthusiasm. She finished high school and entered Southern University in Baton Rouge, Louisiana. During her junior year a recruiter for the Women's Army Corps (WAC) came to the campus and Cadoria subsequently spent the summer of 1960 at Fort McClellan, sampling boot camp. She found that it was extremely hard, but she was intrigued and fascinated by the responsibilities given to young people. Cadoria decided to join the ranks of the lieutenants.

As a black woman in the army, Cadoria encountered many prejudices and hardships. When she sought a protocol job in Vietnam, the recruiter told her she did not have the physical strength to travel and carry luggage. She aptly replied that as a child she had carried hundred-pound bags of cotton and nobody had protested or tried to protect her. Cadoria decided to persevere in the army, hoping that her work would open doors for other black women. Almost every job she did was a first for women in the Army. But Cadoria knew that if her performance was very good, that same job would be given again to a woman, thus advancing their status.

Cadoria served in Vietnam from January 1967 to October 1969. During the grueling months she came to feel that combat was an evil thing, insisting that as human beings we have higher purposes than to kill each other. Nevertheless, Cadoria also says that with their participation in the Vietnam conflict, women proved their suitability for combat. But like their male counterparts they need training. Cadoria adds that if any Army position is closed to women, then the resources of all citizens are not utilized. This is true for a civilian society and for the military environment.

After the atrocities she had witnessed in Vietnam, Cadoria decided to enter a convent upon her return to the United States. Shortly after she returned, however, she received a call from the director of the WAC, congratulating her on making the list for Commanding General Staff College. Cadoria called her mother, who dissuaded her from going to the convent by convincing her that it was her responsibility to all blacks to stay in the Army.

Cadoria did remain in the military, and has continued to lead a brilliant and inspiring career. She has completed important assignments with the Joint Chiefs of Staff, the Law Enforcement Division and the Criminal Investigation Command. In 1985 she became the first black woman to hold the rank of brigadier general. She subsequently became the deputy commanding general and director of mobilization and operations for the Total Army Personnel Agency.

The advice Cadoria gives women about to enter the military is that a woman still has to be prepared to work harder than her male counterparts and be prepared to receive less credit for her efforts. Cadoria has enjoyed her career, however, for she loves the military despite the hardships. There is no shortcut for a black female who becomes a general, but, she says, that should never be a deterrent to any woman.

Jacqueline Cochran

Jacqueline Cochran, affectionately called Jackie by her friends and colleagues, learned to fly during a three-week vacation in the summer of 1932 when aviation was still in its early stages. Her interest in flying was sparked by Floyd Odlum, a banker and industrialist whom Cochran met at a party and who later became her husband. On the third day of her training she was flying alone, taking off from Roosevelt Field in Long Island.

When Cochran completed her training and obtained a pilot's license she decided to become a test pilot. She was surprised to find that all test pilots were men, but this did not daunt her. She would just have to buy her own equipment.

The story of Jacqueline Cochran restores faith in the American dream. She persisted, she worked, she was always honest, and she succeeded. Moreover, she succeeded while she was very young. Cochran was born in 1912 in Pensacola, Florida, now the site of the United States Naval Air Training Command, also known as the Annapolis of the Air. For years she thought herself the daughter of the family she lived with, yet, young as she was, she could not help but observe how different she was from her family. Cochran's family seldom had enough to eat and many times she provided the family pot with a chicken that she "borrowed." When one day little Jackie overheard her "mother" telling another woman that she was not her child but that she had promised never to tell the child her true origins, Cochran only felt relief. The beatings, the dirt, the privations no longer seemed to be her legacy; Cochran could dream now and the revelation strengthened the awesome courage of the little girl. However, it is to her credit that she never abandoned the family that had raised her. She provided for them financially and came to their side when they were sick.

During her childhood Cochran's dresses were discarded flour sacks. She did not attend school, but learned the alphabet by watching boxcars passing by on the rails near her house. Cochran was busy, too, working full time. As a child Cochran did not know that money existed. Her "father" worked, when he could, in the sawmills of Southern Florida. Workers were paid in chips that they exchanged for necessities at the company store. When the mills closed the family had nothing to eat and Cochran begged for the sweet potatoes that farmers cooked for their pigs. If Cochran caught a fish or two, the family dined in luxury.

One of the few things that Cochran knew about her natural parents was that they were Catholic. Her adoptive family never attended any church services, but the mother urged Cochran to go to Mass. The priest in the church she sometimes attended was the first positive influence Cochran encountered in her young life. Another bit of information she somehow obtained was that when she was given to her present family, a tract of land and some oxen had been provided to help with the expenses of her upbringing, but those assets had been lost or sold long ago.

The realization of her complete aloneness was brought home to Cochran at a young age. She was six when she wandered into the woods and got hopelessly lost. No one came to look for her. Overcoming her fear of the shadows and noises of the forest, she eventually made her way home one day later to find that she had not been missed. She was so unhappy that she decided to run away, but where to go? For a while her hopes were pinned on a traveling circus, and the little girl felt betrayed when the circus disappeared in the night leaving her behind.

Cochran had wondered what school was all about, and after

giving it some thought she decided to attend. It could, after all, be no worse than home. But Cochran had not learned to control her temper; rather she used it to defend herself from her parents and siblings. When on the third day of classes the teacher slapped her, Cochran slapped the teacher back and was forced to leave the classroom.

A year later she spied a different teacher in the classroom and decided to try school again. This time she was more fortunate. The teacher taught Cochran not only in school but also at her home. If Cochran brought her firewood, then the teacher would give her ten cents a week. To a child who had never had a penny, ten made her feel rich. Cochran also learned such necessities as basic hygiene from the young teacher. Above all, she learned that she mattered to someone, that the teacher she admired enjoyed her company and was willing to spend time with her.

Cochran was growing more independent and doing a variety of jobs. She helped new mothers by cleaning their houses and caring for their children. Sometimes she was paid, sometimes she was not, but her contribution helped the family.

By the time she was eight years old, Cochran was working a full night shift in a cotton mill, in those days 12 to 14 hours. Her pay was six cents per hour and for the first time she was able to afford some clothes from a peddler and a pair of shoes—the first she had ever worn. But Cochran knew that her determination would win her dreams for her; some day she would be as elegant as her teacher, she would travel, and she would buy the food she wanted. When the mill closed, Cochran found a job in a beauty parlor. The little girl had gumption and would not allow the owner to exploit her, or make her work more and pay her less because of her age. On the other hand, Cochran never shirked her obligations. She was intelligent and hard working, an unbeatable combination, and she learned the new art of giving permanents. Her salary was $1.50 a week plus room and board which she earned by helping the owner with her domestic chores.

Cochran graduated to full pay when she was 13. This came about because when the shop was checked for child labor the owner lied about Cochran's age, adding that the girl was her pupil. Cochran let the statement pass, but no sooner had the inspectors departed than she demanded to be paid as the other workers; after all she was bringing more than $200 a week to the shop.

When Cochran moved to Montgomery to a better job, she met in the beauty parlor a Mrs. Lerton, a prominent citizen of Alabama. Through Lerton, Cochran's horizons expanded. She was introduced to young people, made friends, and attended college parties. Lerton taught Cochran many other useful skills, such as cooking and sewing, and urged Cochran to become a nurse. Cochran did not have a high school diploma, but she studied hard and was admitted into a training program for nurses.

Her strength was in practical nursing, and her performance in the operating room was extraordinary, although she passed all her other subjects as well. Wishing to put her training to good use, Cochran began working for a country doctor. It was like returning to her early years; she was poverty, dirt and hopelessness. She wanted to help people, but she needed to be in a position to do so. In short, she needed money.

The little nest egg she had accumulated bought her a partnership in a beauty parlor, and she used her car to travel rural routes selling patterns and material. Her next stop, with an interlude in Philadelphia, was New York City where she worked in the famous shop of Antoine. She soon found herself in his Miami salon for the winter, a lucky break, for here she met Floyd Odlum, the man she was to marry.

While Cochran was perfecting her flying abilities, her nimble mind realized that not only women but men too bought an enormous amount of cosmetics. Why not get a corner of the business for herself? In Chicago she set up a chemist in a laboratory, and he developed her famous line of cosmetics which became extremely successful.

Although Cochran never neglected her business, her need for money was less pressing and she was able to devote more of her time to her avocation—flying. Cochran tested speed and altitude. The data she collected and brought back were invaluable in developing pressurized craft. She also tested a new fuel in 1939 that was later used during World War II.

Perhaps the hardest part of flying is the one that tests intelligence, reaction time, and quick thinking — unforeseen emergencies. On one occasion Cochran had to do a belly landing, and on another the nose of her craft caught fire and she had to escape from a burning field.

Jackie Cochran was chosen to drive U.S. transport planes loaned to England before the United States became engaged in the war. This led to an unpleasant, *unbelievable* situation for her. Male pilots called a meeting and threatened to strike if women were allowed to fly the planes. They alleged that the Germans would be able to shoot women pilots down with greater ease. In fact, the pilots feared losing prestige if a woman were to do their job.

The outcome was that Cochran was only allowed to fly as first officer; a male pilot would be at the controls during landing and take off. Cochran decided to accept this situation, although she knew, as did the male pilots, that she was as competent as they were.

When the United States Eighth Air Force was being set up in London, Cochran was asked to help in the organization. As the war raged and the need for pilots increased, General Henry "Hap" Arnold asked Cochran to organize women pilots at home. This group became the Women Airforce Service Pilots or WASPs, now no longer in existence.

The cost of training women pilots, Cochran proved, was no higher than the cost of training men, and they flew all types of airplanes with the same efficiency and safety as men.

In 1953 Cochran, piloting a Sabre jet, broke the speed record for men and women. That same year she had the honor of being the first woman to break the sound barrier, and a few years later she was flying at Mach 2. Cochran retired from the Air Force as a colonel and was elected to the Aviation Hall of Fame.

Jackie Cochran died in 1980. Her dreams as a poverty-stricken orphan must have seemed unattainable at times and she could not have envisioned how far she would rise. She never allowed obstacles to deter her, and there were many in her path. Jacqueline Cochran worked hard and never settled for second best.

Rhonda Cornum

The basis for the Persian Gulf War was formed in early August 1990 when Iraqi troops invaded the small nation of Kuwait, repository of 15 percent of the world's oil. U.S. President George Bush joined other world leaders in condemning the invasion. Under the auspices of the United Nations, the United States reacted to the Iraqi invasion by forming a coalition force to restore the Kuwaiti government to power.

One of many women who served with distinction during the Persian Gulf War was Rhonda Cornum. An extremely multifaceted individual, Cornum holds a Ph.D. in biochemistry, was selected as an astronaut candidate, went to airborne school, and is a physician and flight surgeon. With her husband Kory and her daughter Regan, she lives on a farm in Florida where she keeps a dog and five cats and, when time allows, rides horses, runs, cycles, and swims.

Rhonda was born in Dayton, Ohio, but while still small, her parents moved to New York. Though she had two sisters and one brother, the disparity in their ages precluded them from being playmates. However, Cornum's childhood was full; she had a Gordon setter for a pet, and enjoyed riding horses. Young Rhonda seems to have had a very independent personality and a great desire to excel in whatever endeavor she undertook. She attended Wilmington College in Wilmington, Ohio, on a full tuition scholarship. She did splendidly and after two years she left Wilmington to attend Cornell University where she had graduated with a B.S. in microbiology and genetics at 20. Cornum married a botany student and they had a baby daughter, her only child Regan. The young couple was short on money but long on resourcefulness. They kept goats, raised chickens, lived in a small log cabin, used wood for heating, and kept a vegetable garden.

While still at Cornell University, Cornum was asked to speak at a conference in Atlantic City. The topic was amino acid metabolism and her superb presentation attracted the notice of an army colonel who was in the audience. After asking Cornum if she had given the Army any thought as a possible career, he proceeded to inform her that researchers were needed in her field. Cornum had not considered the Army as a possibility, but not long after her presentation she was invited to Fort Letterman and the Army Institute of Research at the Presidio in San Francisco. She was so impressed with what she saw that she enlisted in the army. With her Ph.D. in nutrition and biochemistry, she entered as a first lieutenant and was promoted to captain two months later.

In the Army Rhonda faced complex challenges. Most of the other officers had taken ROTC in college and were conversant in military history, discipline, standard operation procedures, military science, drill and ceremony, and all the many skills that make a soldier. Cornum's background gave her little knowledge of these matters. To complicate matters, she was coping with the ending of her marriage. However, as hard as basic training was, it had its lighter moments. Not having donned a uniform before, Cornum says in her book *She Went to War* (Presidio Press, 1992), that she presented herself at her first formation with her pants on backwards, misled by the side buttons that are used instead of a zipper on women's uniforms.

With boot camp over, she was stationed in San Francisco, where she worked in a laboratory as before. But now her ambition was sharpened; she made up her mind to obtain the Expert Field Medical Badge, which would qualify her for operational medical services in the field. Part of this training is academic and part is practical, but the conditions are field-like and very rough. The women are held to the same rigorous training as the men. Of the 60 people that began the course, she was among the 8 who finished.

The scope of Cornum's research work was hampered by her lack of a medical degree. In fact, she was the only biochemist in the laboratory and was not permitted to do research on humans. Cornum then decided to attain a medical doctoral degree. Already in the Army, she was entitled to attend the Uniformed Services University in Bethesda, Maryland.

It was the right decision in many ways. Not only did she obtain her degree, but she also met her future husband, Kory, whom she married in 1983, and with whom she became a flight surgeon. At first glance it would appear that a doctor is a doctor, and thus capable of caring for anyone. But in reality flight surgeons need to understand altitude physiology, combat medicine, field sanitation and many other disciplines not generally required of physicians. Flight surgeons also learn to fly helicopters and airplanes. Not surprisingly, Cornum graduated first in her class.

Then she began looking for assignments. Her internship was over and her ardent wish was to go to Fort Bragg in North Carolina, the home of the 82nd Airborne, where assignments were available. In fact, the position of battalion surgeon in the aviation brigade of Special Forces would have been ideal for Cornum. But she did not get the assignment — not because she was not qualified or not capable or not willing to do the job, but simply because it was considered a combat position and as such was closed to all women. It was an unpleasant experience to be excluded arbitrarily from a job she knew she could perform. However, Cornum and her husband went instead to Fort Rucker in Alabama and to Eglin Air Force Base in Florida, respectively. The solution to their commuting problem was to settle somewhere in between their two places of work. With this in mind, they purchased a farm roughly equidistant where they enjoyed vacations and weekends.

Cornum's new assignment was as head of Primary Care and Community Medicine at Lyster Army Community Hospital, which meant that she spent most of her time treating civilian dependents. She was soon promoted to major. As always, Rhonda worked hard to have the best primary care unit that could be had, and as always she succeeded. Pilots had her phone number and the knowledge that they could call Dr. Cornum day or night. Civilians felt important and well treated. Then one day, unexpectedly, Lt. Col. Bill Bryan, the battalion's executive officer, asked Cornum if she would like to go to the Gulf, and without hesitation she said yes.

Before departing Major Cornum acquired the appropriate vaccinations, and made sure that all documents were in order. Arrangements needed to be made for her daughter, someone had to care for the animals, and for the thousand and one chores that keep a family and a home going. As a doctor she needed to check all her supplies and equipment. Cornum felt deeply the patriotic desire to do a good job as an officer and a doctor, the need to appear confident before others, especially those under her command, but she also felt the doubts that accompany an expedition into the unknown.

Cornum's journey to the Middle East was complicated and full of stop overs. It began at Fort Benning, Georgia, from where she was taken to Westover, Maryland, and then to the former Torrejón Air Force Base near Madrid, Spain. After an overnight stay at Torrejón, the airplane took her to Dhahran in Saudi Arabia.

August in Saudi Arabia is unbearable with hot temperatures and scorching winds. Military uniforms only add to the discomfort. Nevertheless, work proceeded. The helicopters that had come from the United States disassembled had to be reassembled and made flight worthy. In the meantime, Lieutenant Colonel Bryan, Captain George Hodge and Major Cornum flew to King Fahd International Airport, which was their base for the next few months. The heat here was no less sweltering and the dryness so extreme that soldiers drank ten bottles of water daily to stave off dehydration.

Living conditions were far from luxurious. Personnel lived on the second floor of a concrete parking garage at the airport and slept on canvas cots. Majors and up had the luxury of a whole parking space to themselves. Cornum was the only female officer, but five enlisted women were also there.

Cornum commenced her job by establishing the aid station — a tent in the hangar that was open 24 hours a day. Another worry was added to her many preoccupations when Cornum was informed that her husband Kory had also been assigned to Saudia Arabia exposed to danger.

There were many hardships suffered by all stationed in the Persian Gulf: the daily endurance of unbearable heat during the daylight hours and chilling cold at night, showers with no warm water, latrines with no hand-washing facilities, uniforms worn at all times because Saudi religious beliefs precluded the wearing of shorts and many other casual clothes.

Cornum was assigned to care for the soldiers who conducted helicopter assaults to cut off Iraqi's elite Republican Guard, thus circumventing the major line of defense planned by Iraqi President Saddam Hussein. The prospects for the soldiers were grim, and the expected number of casualties and wounded high. It was predicted that one of four soldiers would be wounded or killed. For most, as for Cornum, this was their first experience in combat.

In due course the battalion left King Fahd airport and the medical corps was installed in a field hospital—a grandiose name for a canvas tent. If attacked their only defense were some Apache helicopters that could not take off in bad weather. For that reason the medical personnel learned to operate the M-60 machine guns. Although they were not allowed to attack the enemy, they could defend themselves and their patients if attacked.

During a seemingly routine mission, Cornum went by helicopter to rescue a pilot who had been shot down. Enemy fire came at them from all directions despite the protective Pathfinder helicopter. Suddenly, from her position on the floor of the craft, Cornum felt the helicopter falling, and then crashing to the sand, rolling over and over and causing her to lose consciousness.

When she came to, Major Cornum found herself unable to move, caught under the fuselage. She began to silently dig in the sand with her legs; her arms had no feeling. Though she saw no one at first, Iraqi soldiers quickly surrounded her. When one bent and grabbed her right arm the pain was so sudden and excruciating that she could not prevent herself from screaming—both her arms were broken. The soldiers lifted her to her feet and kicked her to move her along. But kick as they may, Cornum could move no quicker for one of her knees was badly injured.

The first stop of the little group was a bunker where Cornum was interrogated, though not at length. Then she and another prisoner, Sergeant Troy Dunlap, who had been in the helicopter with

Cornum, were pushed onto a truck, her broken arms swinging with her every move.

Preliminary interrogations over, Cornum and Dunlap were taken to another bunker. So far nothing had been done to ease Cornum's physical suffering. Her arms moved uncontrollably with every motion, and her knee was hurting horribly. She felt weak and nauseous, one of her fingers was crushed, an eye was closed shut with blood, and she was black and blue all over. At the end of the journey that must have seemed interminable to Cornum, she was pushed into a cell.

Being a prisoner is humiliating, being helpless is demoralizing. When she was finally allowed to use the bathroom, a euphemism for a hole in the floor, Cornum had to be helped and undressed by an Arab sentry who subsequently covered her modestly with a huge robe. In her weakened condition, Cornum suffered greatly from the heat of the day and shivered with cold at night. Pain prevented rest and her thoughts returned to the crash, and she wondered about the fate of the rest of the crew.

The next morning Cornum and Dunlap, amid explosions, were driven to a building where a professional translator talked to them. The translator informed Cornum that no doctors were available at the moment, but that efforts to provide one were being made. But, he asked, why had the Americans come to destroy and kill? The Americans did not hate the Iraqi people Cornum replied, and she had come because she was a soldier and must obey.

After a day of waiting, a man entered the room. In her book, Cornum states her belief that he was a medical student for he knew little about medicine. However, he did bandage her arms to her torso, a distinct relief for Cornum. More therapeutic than the treatment were the blankets he supplied. For the first time in days Cornum and Sergeant Dunlap drifted into restful sleep.

When fighting around the area where she was located eased, Cornum, blindfolded as before, was transported to a clinic in Basra. An X-ray revealed the reason for her worrisome weakness and loss of blood—a bullet embedded in her shoulder. Leaving the clinic with her arms splinted, Cornum was placed on a bus. To her surprise she found here the same pilot — bandaged but alive — that she and her crew had set out to rescue. He quietly informed Cornum, for prisoners were not allowed to communicate, that the war had ended. Cornum's elation at the news was tempered by fear; she felt cold and was shivering, an alarming state of affairs for it signaled the beginning of infection that without appropriate medical care could be fatal.

In Baghdad the prisoners were placed in a military hospital. The prisoners were interrogated, knowing that the Iraqis had beaten other prisoners. When Cornum's turn came to answer questions, she supplied her name and rank truthfully, but did her best to convince the interrogator that, as a doctor, she had been kept in the dark about the military plans of the unit. According to the Geneva Convention, name, rank, serial number and date of birth is the only information any captured soldier is obliged to give.

Eventually, the chief of orthopedics at the Rashid Medical Center came to see Cornum and more X-rays were taken. She also had her first bath in five days. It was given in ice-cold water by two Iraqi nurses who had a toothbrush for her. This experience, Cornum confesses, has given her a deeper appreciation for the medical staff — the nurses, therapists, and technicians — so often taken for granted. As a result of the increased physical comfort, Cornum's optimism returned. The doctor asked her if she would consent to surgery. In any case, he would align the bones and place the arms in a cast. Cornum had no reason to doubt the professional competence of the doctor, but she did know that hospital supplies and equipment were decidedly limited, and so chose to wait. When an ophthalmologist assured her that her eye was not damaged, Cornum's thoughts turned to other matters and she began considering how long she would be held prisoner.

Luckily her wait was short. In the middle of the night an attendant came to tell her that she was leaving. To her surprise she was taken to a nice hotel teeming with prisoners surrendered to the International Committee of the Red Cross. Hope surged through Cornum; now she was certain she would be sent home soon. Meanwhile, she basked in the luxuries that the hotel offered: hot water for bathing, conversations with other prisoners, and spaghetti for meals.

In Riyadh the returning prisoners were greeted by General Norman Schwarzkopf. There were pleasant reunions all around. Smiles beamed on emaciated faces. Aboard the aptly named navy hospital ship *Mercy,* Cornum met the doctor, an old acquaintance of hers. And from behind the doctor appeared none other than her husband. Shortly after, Cornum was also talking to her daughter, assuring her that she was alive and well. Cornum spent four days on the *Mercy,* grateful to be alive and cared for, and glad to be surrounded by her husband and friends whom she had at times despaired of ever seeing again.

Then came the day at Walter Reed when awards were given. Despite her pain, Cornum marched up the stage with the others. She was unable to salute, of course, but she stood at attention and did not move a muscle. She was presented a POW medal and a Purple Heart.

Doctors operated on Cornum's arms. A steel rod was placed in her left arm, and a screw in her finger. She was able to give talks and attend meetings, but had to wait until her arms were strong enough to support herself on crutches before having knee surgery. Cornum was well enough to attend the "Victory Award" tea hosted by First Lady Barbara Bush at the White House, and commemorated Pearl Harbor's anniversary at West Point.

In her book, Cornum states that she does not believe in excluding women from combat, nor does she believe that women are going to hinder military performance. As for bonding and troop morale, arguments so often presented by those who oppose women in the military, she saw wonderful examples of both as she worked hand in hand with men doing the same things they did, not as a woman, but as a doctor and an officer.

The contribution of Rhonda Cornum to the war effort in the Persian Gulf was perforce short lived, but the example she set for other women to follow was very important. She proved that men and women can work together in the Army under conditions of great stress and lack of privacy. They work as well-trained members of the U.S. Armed Forces, putting aside all considerations of gender in the defense of their nation. Bonding, albeit situation-specific bonding, occurs and morale is high; the end result is pride in a job well done.

Evelyn P. Foote ──────────────────

Born in Durham, North Carolina, Brigadier General Pat Foote attended Wake Forest University, where she earned a bachelor's degree in sociology in 1953. In 1960, after completing the Women's Army Corps (WAC) Officer Basic Course, she received her commission by direct appointment. From August 1961 to July 1964 she served as the WAC recruiting officer in Portland, Oregon. She then traveled to Fort Belvoir, Virginia, where she became commander of a WAC company consisting of over 250 women from August 1964 to July 1966. In 1966 she completed the Adjutant General Corps Advanced Course.

General Foote then embarked upon a series of important appointments which would later lead to key command and staff positions. From January 1967 to December of that year she was with the U.S. Army in Vietnam, serving as a public affairs officer. She returned to the United States in January of 1968 and was assigned to the U.S.A. Military Personnel Center in Washington, D.C., where she worked as executive officer and company grade assignments officer. She held this post until June 1971. Between 1971 and 1972 General Foote rounded out her military education at the Army Command and General Staff College. In June of 1972 she served in Washington, D.C., with the office of the deputy chief of staff for personnel, as a plans and programs officer for the director, Women's Army Corps. In March of 1974 she left this post to become personnel staff officer at Fort McPherson, Georgia. Two years later she again returned to the classroom, attending the U.S. Army War College until 1977. In November of 1977 she assumed the position of commander, Second Basic Training Battalion, Fort McClellan,

Alabama. She also received a master's degree in public administration from Shippensburg State University.

General Foote then moved to Pennsylvania, where she served from July 1979 to July 1982 as director of personnel management systems in the Command and Management Department of the U.S. Army War College, Carlisle Barracks. In 1980, she graduated from the executive program of the University of Virginia. From July 1982 to March 1983, General Foote studied German at the Foreign Service Institute, Department of State in Arlington, Virginia. Her classes were in preparation for her next assignments: commander of the 42nd Military Police Group, in Mannheim, Germany (June 1983–July 1985) and special assistant to the commanding general, 32nd Army Air Defense Command, in Darmstadt, Germany (August 1985 –May 1986). In June of 1986 General Foote returned to Washington, D.C., to become deputy inspector general, Department of the Army.

During all of these assignments, General Foote proved herself to be hard-working, dedicated and very capable. Some of the numerous accolades and awards for her outstanding service include the Distinguished Service Medal, Legion of Merit (with oak leaf cluster), the Bronze Star, the Meritorious Service Medal (with two oak leaf clusters), Army Commendation Medal (with one oak leaf cluster), Meritorious Unit Citation, National Defense Service Medal, Vietnam Service Medal, the Vietnam Campaign Medal, and the Bundesverdienstkreuz, 1 Klasse (West German Service Cross of the Order of Merit).

In recognition of her abilities, Foote was made deputy commanding general of the U.S. Army Military, District of Washington, a post she held from July 1988 to September 1989. She concurrently held the position of commanding general of Fort Belvoir, Virginia (October 1988–September 1989), a tremendous honor and accomplishment. General Foote became the first woman to command Fort Belvoir and only the second woman to command a U.S. Army base.

Foote is an extraordinary soldier with an impressive record. She said that when she assumed command at Fort Belvoir, she informed all that she intended to serve them with honesty and complete dedication. One of her main concerns was enhancing the quality of life for all those under her command. General Foote firmly believes that if personnel readiness is taken care of, everything else will follow naturally. She hoped that her actions spoke loud and clear of the concern she felt for soldiers, civilians and their families. Foote also made sure that everyone under her command knew that she cared about excellence.

The advice General Foote gives to all soldiers, officers, and civilians comes from a line in William Shakespeare's *Hamlet*: "This above all, to thine own self be true." Foote affirms that in her experience, people who do not compromise their integrity, who are not afraid to stand up for what they believe even when their choices are hard and their decisions unpopular, are the best leaders. People of integrity are dedicated to their jobs and their performance. Foote also emphasizes that without self-discipline no creativity is possible.

On May 15, 1989, Brigadier General Foote was awarded an honorary doctorate degree from her alma mater, Wake Forest University. Dr. Robert M. Helm, head of the military science department at Wake Forest, commented that when General Foote attended Wake Forest, women were not allowed to participate in ROTC. They could only serve in the medical corps of the Women's Army Corps. Foote was extremely competent and she did not hesitate to accept responsibility, he said. Because of what Foote has done in the course of her career, she has become a role model for other women.

The motto of Foote's alma mater is "Pro Humanitate," which in Latin means "for mankind." Foote has never had trouble reconciling this motto with her life's work. According to Foote, one of the functions of the armed forces is to promote peace and whenever possible deter armed conflict. This she sees as being consistent with "Pro Humanitate."

General Foote has helped provide equal opportunities for both men and women, especially African Americans and Hispanics, so that they could obtain responsible positions. It is the hope of General Foote that the example she has set in her professional career will help men and women alike to rise without experiencing the frustration and heartbreak of discrimination. Foote was always viewed by those in her command as being very open and approachable. According to one sergeant, Foote was tough but fair.

General Foote retired from active duty on September 1, 1989. She currently resides in Accokeek, Maryland, but says that she is, even now, ready to aid the Army in any way she can. One way of helping includes the talks she gives on leadership and professionalism in the Army. As she did during her active career, she always stands ready to serve her country.

General Foote has been a trailblazer in a male-dominated field. Her brother, Henry Foote, agrees by saying that to rise as high as she did she had to be better than the men with whom she worked. When Foote was commissioned in 1960, women could only go as far as lieutenant colonel. Since those days, comments General Foote, the opportunities for women in the military have greatly increased. She feels confident that in the future more and more women will be reaching for stars.

Joy Bright Hancock

Joy Bright Hancock, once the highest-ranking woman line officer in the U.S. Navy, led a long and very distinguished military career. She was born in Wildwood, New Jersey, on May 4, 1898. She graduated from Pierce School of Business Administration in Pittsburgh in 1918 and soon thereafter embarked on her Navy career. The United States had decided to enter World War I and Hancock aided in the effort by enlisting as a yeoman first class, in the Naval Reserve. She was first sent to the yards of the New York Shipbuilding Corporation at Camden, New Jersey. She was then promoted to chief yeoman and assigned to Cape May Naval Air Station, also in New Jersey. In September 1919 Hancock left the Navy, but she continued to work at Cape May.

The following year, on October 9, 1920, Hancock married

Lieutenant Charles Gray Little, an American naval aviator who had been decorated with the Navy Cross during World War I. She was widowed a mere 10 months later when the dirigible ZR-2 crashed over the Humber River in England with Lieutenant Little on board.

Hancock then immersed herself in her work, taking classes at Catholic University in Washington, D.C. in preparation for her next position, clerk-secretary in the Navy's Bureau of Aeronautics. She remained in this post until December 1923. Hancock subsequently went on to work as a stenographer and clerk at Lakehurst Naval Air Station in Lakehurst, New Jersey. On June 3, 1924, Hancock remarried, but again her marriage would end tragically. Fifteen months after she wed Commander Lewis Hancock, Jr., a naval aviator and recipient of the Navy Cross, he was killed in the crash of the dirigible USS *Shenandoah.*

Hancock again returned to her studies. She first attended the Paris branch of the New York School of Fine and Applied Arts. She then enrolled in the Henry Berliner Flying School in Washington and earned a pilot's license in 1928. Following that she studied at George Washington University and at the Crawford School of Foreign Service until 1930. Upon completion of her studies, she started work at the Bureau of Aeronautics once again. From 1934 to 1942 she headed the Bureau's editorial and research section. Touted as an authority on naval aeronautics, she wrote *Airplanes in Action* (1938) as well as a multitude of articles in periodicals such as *Flying, Aero Digest,* and *Popular Mechanics.* She also often served as a consultation liaison with the press.

At the outbreak of World War II, Hancock, though a civilian, was an outspoken proponent of legislation to create a woman's naval reserve. When the Women's Reserve of the U.S. Naval Reserve, or WAVES, was finally created by an act of Congress on July 31, 1942, Hancock was one of the first officers to be commissioned. It had not been an easy task to obtain approval for the legislation. It was only after Dean Harriet Elliott of the University of North Carolina wrote to Eleanor Roosevelt that Roosevelt interceded and rapidly obtained presidential approval. On October 15th Hancock was appointed a lieutenant and sent to the Bureau of Aeronautics as representative of the Women's Reserve. Her duties later included acting as special assistant to the deputy chief of naval operations (Air). On August 1, 1943, Hancock christened the destroyer *Lewis Hancock* in honor of her second husband.

In the following year Hancock was promoted twice, to lieutenant commander on November 26, 1943, and to commander on March 5, 1945. On October 23, 1945, Hancock received a Commendation Ribbon from the secretary of the navy, who extolled her crucial role in the development and administration of the program established to integrate women in the naval service.

Hancock rose to the post of assistant director of the WAVES on February 24, 1946, and then on July 26, 1946, became the third and last director of the WAVES, with the rank of captain. Hancock remained in her position until October 15, 1948, when President Harry S Truman declared the war emergency over.

The Congressional act establishing the WAVES did not provide for a peacetime Women's Reserve. Hancock became a leading advocate for such a measure. She informed the Senate that any valuable national defense weapon should be kept in top shape and not permitted to rust or to be destroyed. Hancock then helped draft the Women's Armed Services Integration Act, which was signed by President Truman on June 12, 1948. The Act did away with a separate women's reserve and instead allowed women to obtain regular commissions in the active and reserve divisions of the armed services.

On October 15, 1948, Hancock was one of the first eight women to receive a full commission in the Navy; she held a permanent rank of lieutenant commander. She was also made assistant to the chief of naval personnel, with the temporary rank of captain. Hancock's job was to formulate plans for the peacetime training, utilization, and administration of women in the Navy. On January 11, 1949, she proudly took part in the induction of the first 28 women ensigns at the General Line School in Newport, Rhode Island.

In June 1953 Hancock retired, having earned a Commendation Ribbon, World War I and World War II Victory Medals and a

World War I medal awarded by the state of New Jersey. In 1972 she recounted her myriad adventures and achievements in her autobiography, *Lady in the Navy*. Capt. Joy B. Hancock died on August 30, 1986.

Being among the first to enter a new career field is difficult. It is extraordinarily difficult when you are continually judged by who you are or what you represent and your job performance becomes a tangential matter. As mentioned, Joy Bright Hancock was extremely instrumental in creating the Women's Armed Services Integration Act which elevated the status of military women. Still today, however, true integration has not been achieved, and the work of pioneers such as Captain Hancock continues.

Oveta Culp Hobby

Oveta Culp Hobby accomplished many "firsts" in her life: she was the first woman parliamentarian in the Texas House of Representatives; the first director of the Women's Army Corps during World War II; the first woman to receive the Distinguished Service Medal; and the first person to hold the cabinet position of Secretary of Health, Education and Welfare in a U.S. presidential administration. Although the name Oveta comes from an American Indian name meaning "forget," Oveta Culp Hobby will never be forgotten.

Oveta Culp Hobby was born in Killeen, Texas, on January 19, 1905. Her father was a lawyer-legislator and as a young girl Oveta displayed a precocious interest in politics and public life. As early as age 10, she would spend hours at her father's law office, reading the *Congressional Record* to him.

Oveta went on to study law herself, first at the Mary Hardin-Baylor College in Texas and then at the University of Texas Law School. At age 20 she became parliamentarian for the Texas House of Representatives, serving from 1925 to 1931, and then again from 1939 to 1941. During this time she was also an assistant city attorney in Houston and a legal clerk for the Texas State Banking Commission. As a legal clerk she codified the state banking laws. She was also secretary of the Women's Democratic Club, and was involved in the National Democratic Convention in Houston. In 1928 she unsuccessfully attempted to run for an office in the state legislature. Hobby also found time to write a book, *Mr. Chairman* (published by the Economy Company, Oklahoma City, 1936) which was used to teach school children about parliamentary procedure.

In 1931, after marrying William P. Hobby, a widower 27 years her senior, former governor of Texas (1917–1921), and publisher of the Houston *Post,* Oveta Culp Hobby embarked on a career in journalism. She began as a research editor at the *Post,* and was quickly promoted to book editor. In short order, she held the positions of assistant editor, director and finally executive vice president. She established new sections of the newspaper dedicated to women's news, features which became very popular.

Meanwhile, Hobby continued her involvement in a variety of civic and political causes, including leader of the Texas League of Women Voters and Texas chairperson of the Women's Committee for Mobilization of Human Needs. She was a member of the Junior League Committee on the Constitution and the Women's Committee of the University of Houston Endowment Fund Campaign. Hobby also enjoyed working as director of KPRC radio and television station and as director of the Cleburne National Bank in Texas. With such a multitude of activities, it is little wonder Hobby was often asked how she managed to balance her busy life.

After the start of World War II, Hobby accepted a post in the War Department's Bureau of Public Relations at a salary of only one dollar a year. As the head of the Women's Interest Section, her job was to address the questions and concerns of draftees' wives and mothers.

In September of 1941 Army Chief of Staff George C. Marshall asked Hobby to plan and organize a Women's Army Auxiliary Corps (WAAC) which would exist only until its military worth could be evaluated. On May 15, 1942, President Franklin D. Roosevelt signed Representative Edith Nourse Rogers' bill creating the WAAC.

The next day Secretary of War Henry L. Stimson swore Oveta Culp Hobby in as first director of the WAAC, with rank equivalent to a major.

Hobby's new job soon overtook almost every aspect of her life. She once told a reporter that she would be keeping an eagle eye on the goings-on in Houston but she would be relinquishing all other responsibilities to focus her attention and energy on the WAAC.

One Navy woman stated about Hobby that she made you feel as if all was well with the WAACs — that no problems existed in the Army. The truth was that throughout most of her tenure, Hobby was troubled and frustrated by the Army's disregard and cavalier treatment of the WAAC. Hobby's post — a new director with no precedents or experience to serve as guidelines — would have been difficult enough, but in addition she was placed in the untenable position of being legally reponsible for command of the WAACs without authority or a say in policy decisions. The Services of Supply (SOS) headquarters supervised the WAACs and could veto any of Hobby's proposals.

This almost impossible situation arose from the fact that the WAACs were not a part of the regular Army; therefore, Hobby's title of commander was more a formality than a rank with attendant power. Not only did the WAACs lack the privileges of full Army status, but they were also expected to carry out for themselves such tasks as budget proposals, housing, uniforms and supply, which were performed for the regular Army by experienced agencies. The WAACs, lacking such experience, had difficulty formulating their proposals. Once formulated, the proposals had to be submitted to Army agencies which knew little, and for the most part, cared little about the WAAC's needs and welfare. In addition, Hobby's offices were originally supposed to be part of the general staff, so that she could have access to General Marshall, and thereby gain clout by association and influence with him. In fact, after Hobby accepted the directorship, her office was moved away from those of the general staff.

Hobby was further frustrated when women's enlistment was boosted by lowering eligibility standards. Hobby opposed this trade of quality for quantity. She was borne out when recruitment dropped further due to public opinion that the WAACs were enlisting the lowest elements of society; highly skilled and intelligent women disdained joining such ranks. Officers in the training camps wrote letters to Hobby, complaining about the poor quality of recruits. General Marshall agreed with Hobby and placed her in charge of recruitment. Hobby actively sought highly qualified personnel, but Hobby's reputation, as well as that of the corps, had suffered greatly and enlistment continued to be a problem.

Reform finally came on July 1, 1943, when President Roosevelt signed a bill converting the WAAC to a regular component of the Army. It was renamed the Women's Army Corps (WAC) and Hobby once again served as its director with the rank of colonel. With this new act, recruitment and morale improved, and many of the inequities and confusion were cleared. Nevertheless, some of Hobby's conflicts with the SOS persisted and General Marshall moved her offices to the general staff area, within the office of the Chief of Army Personnel. During her tenure Hobby also argued that WAC volunteers should be treated in the same manner as enlisted men in disciplinary matters. A very controversial issue was that of WACs "pregnant without permission" or PWOP, in which the woman would receive a dishonorable discharge and the man would not be punished. Hobby obtained for these women an honorable discharge and full medical treatment.

Despite the difficulties and obstacles inherent in her position, Hobby was very successful as WAC director for three years. The WACs replaced Army men in about 62 jobs, thus freeing them for combat and duty overseas. The WAC personnel worked as clerks, dental hygienists, cooks, bakers, mechanics, laboratory technicians, administrative personnel, and scores of other positions. Major General Jeanne M. Holm perceptively observes in her book *Women in the Military: An Unfinished Revolution,* (Presidio Press, San Francisco, 1992) however, that the military misguidedly assumed that all able-bodied men were eager to occupy combat positions. They did not take into consideration the doubts or fears harbored by many men who did not want to leave the safety of Stateside assignments and deeply resented being replaced by women so they could be shipped off to battle. Their resentment was unjustly focused on the women, who for their part, had been bombarded by recruiting slogans about their patriotic duty to release the men to fight.

There is no question that Hobby's corps of dedicated women contributed immensely to the United States' success in World War II, and Hobby received national and international acclaim for her leadership. In 1944 she was presented with the U.S. military's highest award for meritorious service, the Distinguished Service Medal.

Hobby had planned to remain WAC director for as long as she was needed, but exhaustion and ill health forced her to resign in July 1945. Her years in office had been extremely demanding. She explained in a statement soon after she retired that any woman in charge of a newly-established corps had to engage in so many battles and provoke so many people that she must inevitably impair her utility to the corps.

Upon her return to Texas, Hobby resumed her work on the Houston *Post,* rising to coordinator and publisher. Continuing her interest in politics, Hobby also became active in the Republican party, serving as a government efficiency consultant to the Hoover Commission and aiding in the election of Dwight D. Eisenhower.

In January 1953 Hobby returned to Washington, D.C., appointed by President Eisenhower to be director of the Federal Security Administration. In March the FSA was abolished and in its place the Department of Health, Education and Welfare was created.

Only the second woman to hold a cabinet position, Hobby was the first Secretary of the Department of Health, Education and Welfare. Under her leadership the Clinical Center of the National Institutes of Health was founded, farmers, domestic workers, and the self-employed became eligible for social security, veterans' benefits were extended, and Dr. Jonas Salk's polio vaccine was produced in great quantity.

In 1955 Hobby returned to the *Post* as president and editor; 10 years later she became chairperson of the board. She turned much of her attention toward radio and television, and in 1976 she was named director of the Corporation for Public Broadcasting. She was much sought-after as a resource and consultant for business corporations, as well as serving on many committees and boards for the Republican Party.

In 1978 the Association of the U.S. Army honored her with its highest award—the George Catlett Marshall Medal for Public Service. The presenter stated that Oveta Culp Hobby, citizen and patriot, had given selflessly of herself, answering her country's every call to duty with honor and courage. This award reflected the achievements of an extraordinary woman.

Grace Murray Hopper

Grace Murray Hopper used to say she had a strong resemblance to the elephant's child in Kipling's *Just So Stories*. The elephant's child was always very curious, always exploring the world. One day the alligator pulled the elephant's child away by the nose, stretching it into the trunk elephants have today.

Hopper's curiosity extended to machines. She always said she loved a good gadget. One time at the family's summer home in New Hampshire she became fascinated with the intricacies of an alarm clock. She decided to take hers apart and see how it worked. When she was not able to put it back together, she went through the house, dismantling six more alarm clocks. After that incident, her family limited her to one clock.

Grace Hopper was born on December 9, 1906, in an era of pioneers. In 1903 Orville and Wilbur Wright flew the first power-driven airplane. In 1908 the first Model T was produced. When Grace was eight Alexander Graham Bell made the first transcontinental phone call. Grace joined the ranks of these famous pioneers as one of the greatest computer scientists in the world.

When Hopper was young, she was confident and inspired, always encouraged by her family to learn. Although it was an unusual idea at the time, Hopper's father felt women should be given the same educational opportunities as men. He was not sure if he could leave his children much money, so he wanted them to be trained and self-sufficient. When Hopper's mother was growing up, she had also been very curious, especially about math, but at the time it was not considered proper for women to study the sciences. By a special arrangement she was able to study geometry, but algebra and trigonometry were forbidden. When Hopper and her sister showed interest and talent in math, Hopper's father was supportive, telling them not to be restricted by societal roles for women.

Grace attended the Graham School and the Schoonmakers School in New York City, where she earned As in math and participated in basketball, field hockey, and water polo. During the summer Grace and her family would go up to their home at Lake Wentworth in Wolfeboro, New Hampshire, where she would enjoy the long summer days playing with her brother, sister, and cousin.

When Grace was ready to enter Vassar College, she failed a Latin exam and was held back for a year. She spent the time studying at Hartridge School in Plainfield, New Jersey, and then enrolled at Vassar in 1924 at age 17. There she studied math, graduating Phi Beta Kappa in 1928. She then received a fellowship to Yale, where she earned a master's degree in math and physics in 1930 and a Ph.D. in math in 1934, the first woman to receive such a degree from Yale. Grace returned to Vassar in 1931 to teach math, rising to associate professor. She also earned another fellowship at New York University, where she studied from 1941 through 1942.

In 1943, as World War II escalated, Gracy Murray Hopper decided to join the WAVES, the Navy Women's Reserve. The Navy discouraged her for a variety of reasons: she was 34 years of age, too old to enlist; she was 16 pounds underweight; and the Navy felt her civilian job as a math professor was already useful in the war effort. Hopper persevered, however, obtaining special permission to enter the Navy and a leave of absence from Vassar. In December 1943 she entered the Midshipman's School at Northampton, Massachusetts, graduating with a commission at the rank of lieutenant junior grade.

Her first assignment: the Bureau of Ordnance Computation Project at Harvard University. Her job was to be the first programmer of the only large-scale digital computer in the world, the Navy's Mark I.

The Mark I was an ugly gadget — a 51-foot-long, 8-foot-high, 8-foot-wide tangle of switches, vacuum tubes and relays — but Hopper was instantly enthralled. Mark I could store 72 words and perform three additions in one second — a veritable marvel at the time.

In the beginning of her programming, Hopper made a lot of mistakes, for the process was tediously repetitive and the computer language unwieldy.

To remedy the problem she built a compiler — a computer program that translates English into machine code that made it much easier and faster for the average person to write a program. In her typically modest way, Hopper shrugged off her achievement, joking that others had not thought of such a system because they did not mind work as much as she did.

Hopper also coined the computer term "bug." One day while working on the computer she traced an error to a moth caught in a relay. She removed the bug and placed it in the daily log book. Since then, any glitch in a computer is called a bug.

In 1946, with the war emergency over, Hopper left active duty. She then resigned from Vassar and went to Harvard as a research fellow in the Computation Laboratory, working as a reserve officer on the Navy's Mark II and Mark III computers. Three years later she went to work for Eckert-Mauchly Computer Corporation in Philadelphia, where she developed the UNIVAC I, the first large-scale commercially available electronic computer. When Remington Rand bought the corporation, renaming it Sperry Rand, Hopper was asked to stay as senior programmer.

In 1952 Hopper and her staff pioneered the use of compilers. While working on it, she had encountered many people who did not see any value to computers. She turned them into converts by explaining that a thing done once is an accident, if done twice it is a coincidence, but if it happens a third time, it is a natural law and must be accepted.

In 1955 Hopper began work on a computer language that could be used in business. She designed it so that a person not mathematically oriented could type in a common phrase such as "subtract income tax from pay" and the computer would translate that into a computer code and perform the calculation. Hopper's program was finished by July 1957 and by 1958 the program, which later came to be known as common-business-oriented language, or COBOL was in circulation. Her COBOL revolutionized business and remains in wide use today. Hopper used to chuckle when asked why she invented COBOL, saying it came about because she was unable to balance her checkbook.

Hopper had meanwhile earned the rank of commander in the Navy. Her intelligence and wit earned the respect and admiration of her Navy programmers, who often referred to her as "Amazing Grace."

She retired from the Navy at the end of 1966 on what she described as a very sad day for her. In less than a year, however, she returned, prompted by the service's lack of standard computer languages. The Navy recalled Hopper to active duty, and assigned her the task of standardizing the various, incompatible computer languages and inducing Navy personnel to use them. She was put on six months' temporary duty, which then turned into many years' duty. In 1973, when Hopper was 71, a special act of Congress was obtained to keep her on active duty. She was made captain in that same year by the chief of naval operations. From 1977 to 1986, she worked as special advisor to the commander, Naval Data Automation Command (NAVOAC).

Much of Hopper's time in the Navy was spent traveling and giving lectures at college campuses and engineering and computer seminars. Her sentinel message was that people should not fear what is new, nor should they be afraid to take chances. She abhorred the concept that the status quo must remain simply because things have always been done a certain way. She felt resistance to change to be the biggest obstacle to progress. In fact, she had a clock on her wall running counterclockwise which told time perfectly—an example of how different is by no means wrong. However, she knew that many people, regrettably, will never change. As a further example of the pioneering spirit, Hopper would tell the story of her ancestor who, during early America, felt his town of Newby, Massachusetts, was becoming too crowded, so he uprooted his family and founded Boscawen, New Hampshire. Hopper advised people to go ahead with their new ideas; apologies can be offered for not obtaining permission, but permission is hard to obtain. She would add that port is not where a ship belongs although there is no doubt that it is safe there.

She claimed that if anyone in the audience said in the next year that things should be left as they always were she would materialize beside them and haunt them for four hours to try to get them to change.

Another trademark of Hopper's lectures was her use of humor to foster an appreciation and understanding of computers which can do calculations in a nanosecond (a billionth of a second). Hopper explained that if she didn't know what a billion was then the people in Washington didn't either. So how could she know what a billionth was? She asked them to please cut off a nanosecond and send it to her.

With that, Hopper would hold up some copper wires, each measuring 11.8 inches, the maximum distance electricity could travel in a billionth of a second. She would then drag out a 984-foot coil, corresponding to a microsecond, the distance electricity could travel in a millionth of a second, and explain that one should hang over the desk of programmers to acquaint them with what they throw away all the time.

Hopper's greatest source of pride was that she was able to train young people, whom she called the United States' greatest resource. She felt young people were not afraid of new technology, and they questioned more and learned more than older people. She would encourage them to explore their capabilities to the fullest extent, to take risks and to try new methods. She would often keep track of them as they got older and remind them that nothing is accomplished without taking chances. She even presented a plan for improving office productivity. In her scheme supervisors would listen to the younger employees, the young employees would keep on going even after having been told "no."

Hopper never forgot to laugh at herself, either. When the original moth that had created a "bug" in her computer was put in a Navy museum, she commented how good it was that the Navy preserves artifacts such as the moth and herself. She would also tell of the time that she was mistaken for an airport security guard, which induced her always to wear the Navy hat in airports. This arrangement was fine until one day an airport worker asked her if she was in the Navy. When she replied, "Yes," he stared at her in shocked silence, finally exclaiming that she must be the oldest person there. In fact, for several years Hopper was the oldest Navy officer on active duty. Her accomplishments impressed Representative Philip Crane of Illinois, who introduced a bill in the U.S. House of Representatives to recognize Hopper's outstanding contributions and to promote her to the rank of commodore. The House passed the bill and President Ronald Reagan appointed Hopper, age 76, a flag officer in the Navy with the rank of commodore. In November 1985, she was promoted to rear admiral.

Two buildings were also erected in Hopper's honor. On September 27, 1985, the Navy Regional Data Automation Center (later the Naval Computer and Telecommunications Station) began work on The Grace Murray Hopper Service Center, which would house a data processing center, training facilities, teleconference and telecommunications rooms, customer service areas, and a museum housing the awards and honors Hopper received. The Hopper Center was built at the Brewster Academy in Wolfeboro, New Hampshire, the site of Hopper's happy summer holidays.

In 1986 the Navy retired Hopper against her will. The ceremony took place on the USS *Constitution* in Boston, where 300 of Hopper's family and friends watched as she was given the defense Distinguished Service Medal, the highest honor awarded by the Department of Defense. Hopper's retirement speech typified her outlook on life, it focused on the future rather than on the past. She urged strong leadership for the young people who would soon assume responsibility for the world.

After her retirement Hopper remained active, working as a senior consultant to Digital Equipment Corporation. She also continued to give lectures, often to standing-room only crowds. She also received many more awards and citations, including the navy Meritorious Service Medal, the Legion of Merit and the National Medal of Technology, presented to her by U.S. President George Bush. She was one of the first women to become a fellow of the Institute of Electrical and Electronic Engineers (IEEE), and to be elected to the National Academy of Engineers. But for Hopper, the biggest award was the opportunity to proudly serve in the U.S. Navy.

Hopper, who had guided the Navy in the computer age, died in Arlington, Virginia, on January 1, 1992. She was buried in Arlington National Cemetery with full military honors.

Joan of Arc

To think of France is to think of a land of plump grapes hanging from vines, of ancient castles, and of fertile green valleys. Yet in the Middle Ages, France was a land of walled cities with muddy, unpaved roads where carts became mired in deep ruts, and where, during hard winters, hungry wolves roamed the streets at night. In this land, doors were barred at sundown and the unlit streets were deserted until sunrise. Holidays, deaths, floods, or the coming of enemies were announced by the distinctive tolling sounds of the church bells. France was very much a country of lore and superstition, where beliefs in fairy trees lingered and wise women expert in potions were feared for their sorcery. This was the France that Joan of Arc knew. It was torn by war; famine and disease were the burden of the overtaxed peasants. King Charles VI suffered from bouts of insanity during which he might, unpredictably, draw his sword and attempt to kill his courtiers. But this was also the time when a king was sacred, for kings were put on the throne by God. To make France's fate more tragic, Queen Isabella was irresponsible, caring not for her country but living solely for her parties and love affairs. The king's younger brother, Duke Louis of Orleans, who practiced black magic if rumor was to be believed, had formed an alliance with his cousin, the Duke of Burgundy, to take the throne from King Charles. In the France of the fifteenth century, the feudal lords had more power and could command more men than the king himself. The Duke of Burgundy was ambitious and wanted no rival. To ensure that none would stand in his way, he ordered his cousin Louis murdered, an act that was not difficult for the Duke of Burgundy's courtiers.

It is said that he who lives by the sword will die by the sword, and shortly thereafter the Duke of Burgundy himself was assassinated. His son Philip — who blamed the king's son, Prince Charles, for the death of his father — declared war on the royal family. Two factions that were to divide France were created — the Royalists or followers of the king, and the Burgundians, who allied themselves with Philip, and eventually with the English.

Across the channel was King Henry of England, a clever and cunning man who carefully watched the developments of France. Surely, he thought, with France torn by civil war, England could easily annex that territory for the crown. Thus, in 1415, King Henry landed in France and started what was later called "The Hundred-Year War." With Queen Isabella on his side, it was easy for Philip, now the Duke of Burgundy, to persuade the mad king to join their enterprise. To avoid future threats, they contrived to have the king's son, Prince Charles, disinherited.

When the English settled in Normandy, Duke Philip was given the government of Paris. Shortly thereafter an outbreak of the black death spread disease and death throughout the country. So many people died that it became impossible to bury all, and wolves at night and dogs during the day fed on the deceased. In abject fear, many peasants turned to witchcraft and the church, afraid of heresy, instituted investigations. Many of those accused of witchcraft, although little or no evidence may have been found against them, were put to death in the only fitting way to kill a witch — by burning at the stake.

In the meantime, Prince Charles, the Dauphin as the heir to the crown of France is called, was living in exile. He did not have the money to pay an army, nor the power to summon a great number of men. The English on the other hand, commanded large numbers of troops. Moreover, they could count on the help of the Duke of Burgundy. The town of Orleans, under British siege for many months, deprived of resources and leadership, was ready to surrender to the English.

The Middle Ages were a time when few men and fewer women could read and write, certainly no peasant girl was expected to have any schooling. A woman had to obey her parents as a child, her husband when she married, and the church at all times. She must be faithful and devout, fast during Lent, attend Mass and say her prayers, which she could then teach to her children. In this context it is even surprising that the girl who defeated the powerful English army was born to a peasant family living near the village of Domremy on the border between Lorraine and Champagne by the river Meuse.

Joan of Arc was born in 1412. She had a sister and three brothers. The family lived in a stonehouse and was better off than many, for Joan's father was a tax collector for the local lord. Joan's house was similar to most peasant cottages. There was a fairly large common room where the parents slept. It was here that the food was cooked and eaten, the mending and sewing done, and the family gathered on wintry nights to tell stories of ghosts and haunts. The boys slept in the loft, and Joan and her sister had a tiny room off the common room. They possessed few earthly goods and knew the hour of the day by looking at the sun. Any emergency or disaster was announced by the sound of the bells in the church tower. Joan and her family worked hard in the fields. Boars and wolves inhabited the nearby woods, making them very dangerous. During hard winter nights the hungry wolves roamed the village streets while the villagers quaked behind barred doors.

Because France was divided, one village might be loyal to the king and the next might have pledged allegiance to the Burgundian cause. Thieves and brigands, taking advantage of the confusion, looted one and the other. As it happened, Joan's village and her family were loyalists.

But it was not all toil and fear in Joan's childhood. After the harvest was collected, the villagers had picnics in the early autumn sun in the clearings near the village. They danced around the "fairie trees," an old custom dating back to pagan times when it was thought that spirits inhabited the trees. Merry, too, was the coming of the peddler, once or twice a year, hoisting his huge pack along. Through him the villagers knew what had happened in faraway corners of France and how their cause was faring in the war. It was the pack peddler who informed the village that the little island of Mont Saint Michel had stood off the English.

This was of special significance to Joan because Saint Michel was the patron saint of the royal family and of her own village of Domremy. This news must have seemed like an omen of good things to come to young Joan. In any case, shortly after learning what had happened to Mont Saint Michel, Joan heard the first of many voices that guided and consoled her throughout the rest of her short life. The voice was always accompanied by a bright light. Sometimes Joan was sure that it was the voice of St. Michel, but she was afraid of not being believed and so told no one. The first voice told Joan to be a good girl and assured her of God's guidance. For the rest of her life, Joan was convinced that the voices came from God and she obeyed them implicitly. She never preached on matters of dogma and never presumed to have any supernatural powers. Indeed, she laughed at those who claimed she did.

Joan's parents must have sensed something strange in their daughter, for her father saw her amidst soldiers in his dreams and hastened to arrange a marriage for her. But Joan refused, thus not only disobeying her parents, a grievous enough offense, but defying the conventions of the community. Now Joan knew that she must leave her home if she were to follow the dictates of the voices, a most difficult endeavor. Young unmarried women were carefully guarded and Joan had neither money nor possessions to aid her. However, luck was with her for a cousin who was expecting a baby asked for help and Joan's parents consented to let her travel to Vaucoulers.

Quoting to her cousin's husband the prophesy that "France would be lost by a woman [Queen Isabella] and saved by a virgin [Joan]," and making good use of her charismatic and magnetic personality, she succeeded in being introduced to the governor of Vaucoulers, Robert de Baudricort. Perhaps Joan wished to know a man who was influential and she knew that de Baudricort was loyal to the Dauphin and therefore an enemy of the queen and of the English. Or perhaps Joan had hoped to convince him of her divine mission. In any case, the governor laughed at this peasant girl who thought she could recover France for the Dauphin where knights had failed. But her voices continued to reassure her and she did not despair. Only now she told her missions to all who would listen. At first no one paid attention to Joan, but the medieval mind was conditioned to believe firmly in the spiritual.

Joan's fame spread so much that the Duke of Lorraine asked to see Joan. He was a Burgundian and Joan did not want to go, but a peasant could not disregard the summons of a lord so Joan obeyed his command and appeared before him. It was a great disappointment for the young girl as the sick old man did not wish to hear of her mission, but instead hoped that Joan had the power to cure him. Joan denied that she had any supernatural powers and quickly let him know that she could not perform a miracle on his behalf.

At about this same time, Joan learned through her voices that the French had just been defeated by the English and she proclaimed this information in the village square. When the official news arrived days later, confirming Joan's prior knowledge, her fame soared. Yet there were doubts. Was Joan guided by God or was she an instrument of the devil, who everyone knew could adopt any guise to deceive and confuse true believers. To be completely sure, de Baudricort had Joan exorcised.

And so it was that in February of 1429 Joan set forth to see the Dauphin. She wore male attire and rode a horse she had received from a peasant. Her group of followers consisted of eight people. The Dauphin lived 350 miles away, a short journey by today's standards but a gruesome distance in Joan's day. The group traveled in rain and sun and forded rivers swollen with the spring floods, all the while wary of the ever-present menace of bandits. When crossing enemy territory, Joan had to be especially careful for she knew that her fame had reached the ears of the English.

As soon as the caravan was close to Charles's castle and in a loyalist town, Joan rushed to church to thank God for her safe journey. She then took time to dictate a letter to the Dauphin announcing her arrival and explaining the reasons why it was imperative that she be given an audience. When at last she was granted the interview, Joan tried to impress her urgency upon the indecisive, weak, sleepy-looking Dauphin. "For it has been revealed to me that I have a little over a year to live," she told him. But before she died, Joan swore to the Dauphin, he would be crowned the rightful king of France. However, the English must be defeated first and for this she needed his help.

The king's council, many of whom were self-seeking, corrupt men, took precious time to debate whether Joan was a tool of the devil and therefore a weapon of the English, or whether she was what she pretended to be, the savior sent by God. The only way to make sure was to have Joan examined by priests, as the devil would then reveal his presence. To this end, Joan was questioned for weeks as the clergymen were worried about the voices Joan professed to hear. At last, the clergymen cleared Joan of dealings with the devil, and they advised the Dauphin to allow her to help lead the loyal troops to Orleans.

Joan was beside herself with joy. Wishing to avoid fighting if at all possible, Joan dictated a letter to the English asking them to surrender to the "maid sent by God." Needless to say, she received no reply.

The young girl had changed considerably since she had left her village. She wore full armor, never left her male dress and always carried a sword. The sword came to her in a miraculous way. Stopping to pray to St. Catherine in the Chapel at Fierbois, she dreamt that a sword was buried by the altar. And indeed the sword was there.

When Joan arrived at Orleans she found that the thick stone walls surrounding the city were 30 feet high. The city was so well protected that even after many months of siege it had not yet surrendered to the combined English and Burgundian forces. Despite all the fighting the French had managed to keep an access to the city open through which all supplies entered. But now the English were a mere mile from the gate and had fortified an old church from which they planned to stop any supplies from reaching the city. A powerful new weapon, the canon, was aiding long-range attack, inflicting heavy casualties and causing vast damage. The besieged responded from the city walls by throwing hot oil and water on the attackers, along with burning torches and spiked iron balls. The English had another enemy within them — fear. Whether a saint or a witch, through sorcery or miracles, Joan was a threat to their plans of conquest.

Meanwhile, Joan was greeted by Count Dunois of the city of Orleans. Joan expressed her urgency to him. But Count Dunois refused to attack the English until all the boats laden with cattle, fodder, and supplies were safely unloaded and in the city. This infuriated Joan. For three days she waited, praying, trying to reconcile the urging of her voices with the delaying tactics of Count Dunois.

Finally, the Count returned to the city with reinforcements, but he was also the bearer of bad news. The English too were expecting reinforcements, thus once more they would have a greater number of troops than the French. Joan knew she had to attack immediately. The attack finally began, but it went badly for the French. In full retreat to the haven of the city walls, they caught sight of Joan riding boldly and extolling the men to greater effort, imbuing a renewed spirit into the soldiers. They turned back to face the enemy and forced the English to retreat, taking their stronghold and leaving many enemy dead on the field. This had been the first French victory in a very long time, and it proved that the English were not invincible. The confidence of the French, waning during so many fateful encounters, was restored.

Joan was not a strategist or she would have pressed her advantage. But why Count Dunois did not take advantage of the situation is a mystery. Perhaps it was Joan's devoutness that influenced the decision that no fighting should take place on Ascension Day. Surely she felt that it must be celebrated and the fighting men must be given a chance to make their peace with God. Whatever the cause, the respite provided the French much needed rest. And the day after the feast of the Ascension fighting began anew. Joan rode in the midst of the men, inspiring them with such certainty of victory that the English were forced to retreat to the Tourelles, the fortified towers located at the south end of the bridge to Orleans.

Joan was overjoyed at the victory but nearly cried in frustration when Count Dunois deemed that their force was not large enough to carry the attack to the Tourelles itself. Joan knew differently; her voices had insisted that she press the attack. Her position was a difficult one, for great as her prestige and fame were in the councils of war, she had no official authority nor was she ever put in command. Joan knew from her voices that she herself would suffer a wound the next day. When an arrow penetrated her left shoulder, her fame of prophesy reached its highest point. As always, Joan herself declined possessing any supernatural powers; her voices, sent from God to aid the just cause of France's freedom, had told her what to expect.

How could she disobey the voices? It was better to disobey those on earth. Deciding to bypass the decision of Count Dunois, she gathered all who would follow and set out for the Tourelles. The bailiff attempted to stop her — his orders allowed no one to leave the city — but he had to stand aside or be trampled.

After 14 hours of continuous fighting, Joan and the soldiers were exhausted. Suddenly Joan was pierced by an English arrow and was taken aside to assess the gravity of her wound. No sooner was a dressing applied, than Joan mounted her horse and rode undaunted among the men exhorting them to victory. While this battle was raging on one side of the Tourelles, the people of the city were constructing a portable bridge to span the gap that had been created by a cannon shot in the stone bridge that led to the north side of the walls of the Tourelle. With whatever weapons they could gather, ranging from hoes to thick branches to pitchforks, the citizens of Orleans invaded the tower. When the English who were fighting outside of the walls of the Tourelle attempted to seek shelter within, they found themselves being attacked from inside. Moreover, the French set fire to the wooden drawbridge and a great number of soldiers fell into the moat and drowned, unable to swim because of the weight of the armor they wore.

After the victory the popular acclaim of Joan reached its apogee. All were sure she was a saint, with powers to heal and to work miracles if only she would. Again and again Joan denied having any powers and would not attempt to work any miracles. What little she had done had been under the guidance of her voices; if she had any merit it was simply that of believing in God and obeying Him. Try as she might to dispel all rumors of her supernatural powers, the people were in no mood to believe her.

Aware of the short time left to her on earth, Joan proceeded with her campaign. The next step was to be the coronation of the Dauphin as king of France. Joan was certain that France would become united under him. Denied help from the Burgundians, the English invaders would have to abandon her country.

The irresolute Dauphin was doubtful. He believed in moving slowly and was afraid to anger the Duke of Burgundy. Such anger might spur the Duke into further action against him. Furthermore, the King had no money, whereas the Duke's treasury had been enriched by contributions from the English. Joan begged the Dauphin time and again until at last he agreed to march to the cathedral at Reims for this coronation. Anew Joan explained to Charles the need to hurry; again and again her voices warned her that she had little over a year to live.

On the way to Reims Joan and her band of knights and soldiers conquered still one other town, Jargeau, for the Dauphin. The soldiers were eager to jump to the fray with Joan thinking that if she were with them nothing could harm them. She was their God-sent messenger and protector.

There are many mysteries that surround Joan and it is hard to separate fact from fiction. After all, the writing of her contemporaries is colored by political considerations and by superstition. But some things are very intriguing. In the midst of the battle at Jargeau, Joan had another of her premonitory visions. With cannon roaring in her ears, Joan rushed to a knight and shouted to him to get out of the way for a cannonball would tear him apart if he failed to obey her. The confused, frightened knight moved from the spot and just as he reached safety, a cannonball landed on the very place he had stood upon, blowing into pieces the unfortunate man who had taken his place. Why was this particular knight chosen for life?

By now Joan's fame had spread throughout the land. What was the reaction of Joan's family and her village? It is known that men came from distant parts to join the army and their numbers increased the power of the French. Pressing her advantage, Joan conquered two more towns from the English. At this time the French were learning modern warfare. Before now it was thought chivalrous to let the enemy prepare fully and get ready before engaging in battle. Now an element of surprise had aided Joan in several battles, and the soldiers quickly understood the advantages of catching the enemy unawares. So they left behind the old ways and cut their combat losses greatly.

When the Dauphin arrived at Reims with his entourage, the town prepared to hold the coronation the very next day, a Sunday. Times were hard, food and supplies scarce, and the people of Reims were in no position to have the whole royal company as guests of the city for long. Thus on July 17, 1429, in Reims Cathedral, the Dauphin Charles was crowned king of France after taking the sacred oath to defend the faith and the church and to administer justice to his subjects. Joan, tall and proud, waited beside the monarch, happy that she had made this moment come true.

Her voices had told Joan that her fall was near, and she also knew that it would be caused by others than herself. For this reason she tried to convince the king to march on Paris, which could be easily taken now. However, Joan was too naïve in diplomatic matters to be aware of the moves being made without her knowledge. Charles had signed a truce with the Duke of Burgundy. Not only once, but twice King Charles gave his enemies time to prepare Paris to resist through treaties or truces. Had Charles followed Joan's advice it seems extremely possible that the city of Paris would have been taken with a minimum of losses. Also, the rich ransoms collected from powerful captives would have gone a long way in replenishing the coffers of the king. Alas it was not to be.

The city of Paris was surrounded by thick and sturdy stone walls, and those were surrounded by a deep moat and a ditch—all formidable obstacles to ward off attack. By the time Charles was ready to launch the battle for the city, the army was demoralized and Joan frustrated. By nightfall of the first day of fighting, when Joan would have pressed on, she was forced to pause. The next day, as Joan and the troops were launching their attack, orders came from the king which none dared disobey, commanding Joan to desist on her attack and return to the encampment. In the eyes of the simple men, Joan had failed to lead them into victory, no matter for what reasons. Sad and uncomprehending, Joan accompanied Charles and his court for several months, knowing that each day brought her end a little closer and fearing that she would not be allowed to complete her mission and to free France of foreign interference. Occasionally she was allowed to fight to take a town in the name of the king, but lacking men and supplies, her second attempt at liberating a town was unsuccessful. With her disillusioned little band of fighters, Joan retreated to a town near Compiegne, loyal to Charles. When she learned that the Duke of Burgundy was gathering men to attack Compiegne, she rushed her pitifully small band to the town's rescue.

The battle was hand-to-hand combat. The Duke had the advantage—he could summon reinforcements at will and Joan could not. Because of the overwhelmingly large numbers in the field, Joan's men panicked and ran for the security of the walls of Compiegne. The attack was stemmed but in their hurry the fleeing men lifted the drawbridge leaving Joan and some others in the field. It wasn't long before Joan and her men were caught. This was a moment of jubilation for the Burgundians and for the English; Joan, the living legend, was in their power.

Though prisoners of rank were given to the highest officials, Joan was given to a vassal of the Duke of Burgundy, Jean de Luxembourg who put her in his castle at Beaulieu. Several people wanted to buy her, among them Bishop Cauchon, a former member of the

University of Paris and a theologian of renown. The man who should have ransomed her, who owed the crown to her, did nothing. King Charles, fearful and cowardly, stood by and washed his hands of Joan. The people of France loved Joan, cried and prayed for her, and cursed her jailers, but they had no political power. It is not that Joan was badly treated, at least in the beginning. The de Luxembourg family visited with her, she was allowed to take walks on her tower and the family tried to prevent her being sold to the English. Soon however Joan was handed over. In desperation, Joan, who had already once before attempted to escape without success, jumped from her 70-foot high prison tower to the ground. She knew that suicide was a mortal sin and it was not clear to her why God had not punished her sinfulness by killing her. It was clear to her enemies — the devil had carried her body down and not a single bone was broken. What better propaganda could her enemies claim for Joan's supposed witchcraft practices?

The English desired to preserve the appearance of a just trial, and they agreed that Joan be tried by Bishop Cauchon and other theologians from the University of Paris. She was accused of sorcery, heresy and witchcraft, along with other charges such as attempting to raise herself above the authority of the Church by claiming her voices were direct mandates from God. She was held in chains, and was denied her request to be sent to a church prison. It is to the shame of the judges that Joan was treated as a common criminal, that they allowed the jailers to harass her, and that her trial was unfair, a political ploy on the part of the Burgundians and the English. More shameful was Charles' behavior, for he never broke his silence to help her.

No evidence was found against Joan and several churchmen criticized the trial. One who dared to speak was arrested; another had to flee. Finally, Bishop Cauchon called in the Inquisition. Even members of this institution were unwilling to lend themselves to the bishop's machinations. But there were those who through fear or hopes of gain agreed to form part of the tribunal whose clear, if unstated, mission was to ensure that Joan ceased to exist.

Joan's prosecutor, Jean d'Estivet, never let an opportunity go by without personally attacking Joan, who had no counselor or defender and was allowed to call no witnesses. In fifteenth century France an accused was considered guilty until proven innocent. The tribunal was most insistent on the matter of witchcraft for by proving that she had obtained Charles's crown by machinations with the devil, the coronation could be declared null and the English king could reign in France.

During the three months of the trial, Joan was not permitted to attend Mass nor was she allowed confession. She never saw her family. Joan swore to tell the truth, but she reserved the right to answer questions that had to do with God's revelations, sometimes only postponing the answer until she received permission from her voices. Yet the judges seemed unshaken in their determination to prove that the voices came from the devil. Finally, worn down by never-ending repetition, Joan revealed that one of the voices was that of St. Catherine, the other was St. Margaret, and the third was St. Michel. With no evidence of witchcraft, the English feared that Joan might be freed. To this end, they drafted a contract stipulating that at the end of the trial Joan would be turned over to them. The contract also absolved the judges should any criticism of the trial ensue.

The judges did all they could to obtain a confession. They transported Joan to the dungeons where the torture instruments were stored. But even the sight of these inhuman machines failed. Joan did not contradict herself, rather she asserted time and again that she was a good Catholic.

The English were growing impatient. Delays were not good for their cause, especially when Joan failed to recant. Bishop Cauchon then decided to end the trial, condemning Joan to life imprisonment, again denying her transfer to a church prison. However, the English were not happy with the verdict. They wanted the threat that Joan represented removed forever. To please them, the sentence was changed—Joan would be burned at the stake. Once again, history is unclear as to the exact happenings, but the infraction on which the change of sentence was based seems to be that Joan had consented to wear feminine apparel but one night, she said, as she lay asleep her clothes were removed and her male attire tossed into the cell. No doubt if this ploy had failed, another would have succeeded, and yet there is an obvious contradiction for Joan was allowed confession and communion before being sent to her death. Surely a witch would not have been given either.

Joan accused Bishop Cauchon directly of being the instrument of her death. History does not describe his sentiments at that time, but he did nothing to save Joan. Just a young girl, Joan broke and cried before her execution; to increase her shame she was made to wear on her shaved head a cap with her alleged sins written on it. Nevertheless she kneeled down and asked forgiveness for her executioners.

The mob at the stake was enormous. Some came to pray for Joan, many more to witness a spectacle that would enliven their dull existence. Some shouted that a saint was being burned, others just shouted.

Joan of Arc's efforts, her victories, and her sacrifice had changed the history of the country she held so dear. Two years after her death the English left France forever. And in 1456, Joan was posthumously acquitted by the Catholic Church. This brave young woman was canonized in 1920 and stands today as the symbol of freedom from foreign oppression.

Mildred McAfee (Horton)————————

Mildred McAfee, born into a family of educators and Navy personnel, went on to become an outstanding educator and Naval officer herself. She was born in Missouri on May 12, 1900, on the campus of a college her grandfather had founded, Park College. She eagerly embraced an academic lifestyle, for, she maintained, a liberal education is a privilege. McAfee attended Vassar and received a B.A. in English and economics in 1920.

McAfee then launched into an extremely successful career in teaching and administration, receiving promotions almost yearly.

Upon her graduation from Vassar, McAfee accepted a position as teacher in French and English at Monticello Seminary in Godfrey, Illinois. The following year she became an eighth grade assistant at Francis Parker School in Chicago. In 1922 the Fourth Presbyterian Church in Chicago made her director of girls' work. In 1923 McAfee joined Tusculum College in Tennessee as acting professor of economics and sociology. McAfee then went on to become dean of women and professor of sociology at Centre College in Kentucky, from 1927 to 1932. During this time she also attended the University of Chicago, earning an master of arts degree in sociology and anthropology in 1928. McAfee also became executive secretary of the Associate Alumnae of Vassar College, a position she held from 1932 to 1934. In 1934 she was made dean of women at Oberlin College. Finally, in 1936 McAfee became president of Wellesley College. She was 36 years old.

Selected by the trustees of Wellesley College after a rigorous one-month search, McAfee soon proved to be an excellent choice for president. Making only minor innovations, "Miss Mac," as she was affectionately known to most of her students, maintained the stability and tradition of Wellesley with firm leadership. McAfee also earned the respect and admiration of other educators, who showered her with honorary degrees, from Oberlin, Goucher, Wilson and Williams Colleges, Mt. Holyoke, Bates and Boston and Wesleyan Universities.

McAfee continued to be a staunch, outspoken supporter of education. She firmly maintained that society needs men and women who are knowledgeable in a variety of fields and who have developed their intellectual talents to help solve the difficult problems which confront us all. McAfee also strongly upheld equality between men and women. She believed that the world would one day realize that life would be greatly improved if every person were permitted to fulfill whatever role their unique talents indicated without regard to gender. Today we can appreciate better McAfee's position on sex discrimination and wrest it, at least partially, from a utopian view precisely because of people like her.

McAfee's idyllic academic life was interrupted when the

United States entered World War II. President Roosevelt signed a bill establishing the Women's Reserve in the Navy on July 30, 1942, and prevailed upon McAfee to be the director. It was not the first time McAfee had served her country; while at Vassar she had interrupted her studies during World War I to go to Washington, D.C., for a one-week job, pasting clippings in scrapbooks. Several of her ancestors had fought in the War of 1812 under Commodore Matthew Perry.

McAfee, known as Captain Mac, already knew quite a bit about the women's reserves. She had served on the Educational Advisory Committee for the Navy Training Program which had helped establish the Women's Reserve. McAfee immediately put her considerable experience and organizational skills to work. She felt that women's call to duty in the war was a matter of a job that needed doing and therefore did not want any special names or distinctions for the women in the navy. They would simply be citizens aiding in the war effort. However, after a Washington newspaper called the women "gobletts," Captain McAfee gave reluctant agreement to the acronym WAVES (Women Appointed for Volunteer Emergency Service).

Captain McAfee's task — to recruit, organize, and train women to fill a variety of technical and administrative posts so that men could be freed for active duty overseas and in combat — was not an easy one. Although sworn in on August 3, 1942, as a lieutenant commander in the Naval Reserve, the highest rank under the law, she possessed little real authority and many senior naval officers distrusted her. Captain McAfee's true power was only "borrowed"; the WAVES office was in the Bureau of Naval Personnel and the bureau chief, Rear Admiral Randall Jacobs, provided any clout Captain McAfee required in enacting policies.

In addition to making use of such borrowed power, Captain McAfee created a network of female officers, placing an officer in each staff agency of the Bureau of Personnel. She would then hold an informal morning coffee hour known as "Captain Mac's coffee klatsch," during which the women in the different agencies could bring up any problems they had encountered and receive support, information, and suggestions from the others. In this way, the women could help each other and therefore the war effort. Captain McAfee was soon given the title Special Assistant to the Chief of Naval Personnel for Women and, together with her all-woman staff of lieutenants, lieutenants junior grade and ensigns, she successfully led the WAVES in the wartime years.

Unfortunately, despite the women's valuable contributions, many male naval officers' mistrust and resentment toward women remained unchanged. Essentially they felt that the women were invading their territory. This biased attitude even extended to the uniform created for the women. In contrast to the men's sober uniform with gold stripes, McAfee felt that the women's uniforms resembled a comic opera costume with red, white, and blue stripes. The Navy refused to allow women to wear gold stripes, but McAfee was able to convince them, at least, to use light blue braid on the women's uniforms and dispense with the tri-colors. Later, McAfee stated that the whole incident was a big slap in the face, although at the time she did not know enough about Navy dress to realize the superiority that those gold stripes represented. When women entered active duty after World War II, the Navy finally gave women their due and allowed them to wear the gold. The WAVES design was otherwise very practical and popular, and, with minor changes, is the uniform used today.

Early in 1946, Captain McAfee left the Navy and resumed her academic life at Wellesley. She enjoyed being able to spend more time with her husband, the Reverend Douglas Horton, whom she had married in August 1945. McAfee remained president of Wellesley until 1949, when she became president of the National Social Welfare Assembly, a post which she held for three years (1950–1953). In 1959 Captain McAfee turned her interest abroad, serving until 1961 as president of the American Board of Commissioners for Foreign Missions. In 1962 she was a delegate to the United Nations Educational, Scientific, and Cultural Organization (UNESCO). The issue of women's rights remained of paramount importance for Captain McAfee, and in 1963 and 1964 she was co-chair of the National Women's Commission on Civil Rights.

Captain McAfee's intelligence, courage, sense of humor and

resourcefulness made her a legendary figure in her time and an inspiration for future service men and women. She died on September 2, 1994, in Berlin, New Hampshire. She was 94 years old.

Geraldine Pratt May

At 5 feet, 3 inches, Colonel Geraldine Pratt May was diminutive in size, but not in courage or vision. "Jerry" (or "Gerry") as she was known to her friends, was born on April 21, 1892, in Albany, New York, but grew up in Tacoma, Washington. An avid sportswoman, she enjoyed summer camp, where she could swim and play tennis. She continued her athletic pursuits in college and became president of the women's athletic club at the University of California at Berkeley. May also devoted herself to her studies and in 1920 graduated from Berkeley with a B.A. in social economics.

May's first job was as a social worker in San Francisco, where she was involved in Americanization activities. She then worked in Sacramento, first in the recreation department, and then as an officer of the Camp Fire Girls. She spent five and a half very enjoyable years training camp counselors and running the summer camp. In 1928 she married Albert E. May, a contractor, and gave up her job to become a fulltime homemaker. She and her husband moved to Oklahoma, where they lived for more than ten years, until California beckoned them back. May's husband died in California in 1945.

May's military career started in July 1942 when she joined the women's auxiliary of the U.S. Army. She was in the first class of women to graduate from the Women's Army Auxiliary Corps (WAAC) officer candidate class at Des Moines, Iowa. Second Lieutenant May started her active duty as a recruiting officer, working for five months for the Recruiting District of Oklahoma. She then became one of the first 18 Women's Army Corps' (WAC) officers to enter the U.S. Army Air Force. Although she was older than the maximum age limit for assignment to the regular Air Force, May

entered the active reserve and in March 1943 was appointed WAC
Staff Advisor for the Air Transport Command (ATC). Her gentle
nature belied her strong leadership qualities and sometimes fooled
people into thinking she was too mild-mannered to be an effective
military officer. In fact, when her appointment was announced,
Secretary of the Air Force Stuart Symington Huntley informed her
that she was not his first choice.

May proved to be an excellent choice, however. Her new duties
entailed advising the chief of staff and the air staff on policies concerning the WAC. She also spoke to commanders and made recom-
mendations concerning the training, duties, and welfare of women
under their command. May oversaw over 6,000 WAC officers and
enlisted personnel on 41 different bases throughout the world. Part
of her duties was to inspect these bases and ensure that they were
appropriate for WAC personnel. She received a promotion to captain in April of 1943, to major in November of the same year,
and to lieutenant colonel on May 31, 1945. May continued her work
as the WAC Staff Advisor for the ATC until the summer of 1946
when she joined the War Department's general staff in Washington, D.C.

Lieutenant Colonel May's dedication and hard work earned her
the position of WAC staff director with the Army ground forces stationed at Fort Monroe, Virginia. From 1947 until 1948 she oversaw
all WAC officers and enlisted personnel in the six Armies. She was
then assigned to the War Department; working with the Office of
the Executive for Reserve and the Reserve Officers' Training Corps
(ROTC) in establishing a program for the WAC in the reserves.

On June 12, 1948, the Women's Armed Services Integration
Act became a law; women in the Air Force (WAF) were now a part
of the regular Air Force.

No one could have been more suitable to lead the WAF than
May. On June 14, 1948, May became the first Director of Women
in the Air Force, with the rank of colonel. She now had responsibility for the administration and management of all women in the
Air Force. The response from U.S. women to the new law allowing
women to be part of the regular Air Force was overwhelming — some

hopeful enlistees were turned away because the law permitted a set number of women in the Air Force. May then determined which Air Force tasks women and men could do equally well, which could be done better by women, and which could be done better by men. In this way she hoped the United States could be better prepared for war.

May's tenure was unfortunately fraught with tension and dissent. As the Air Force moved towards integration, it wanted to end the supervision of enlisted women by WAF officers; instead enlisted women would be supervised under the same male-dominated structure responsible for supervision of the enlisted men. May vigorously opposed such a movement. She feared that the enlisted women's welfare might suffer and their issues would be ignored amidst the massive male structure. Also the WAF commissioned officers provided valuable role models for the young women enlistees which they otherwise would not have.

In 1950 the chief of staff, General Hoyt S. Vandenberg, expressed his displeasure with the WAF but refused to speak with May. Instead he sought counsel from people who knew less about the WAF than May, thus creating chaos among the Air Force women and causing May to resign in June of 1951.

May received two decorations for her contributions during World War II — the Legion of Merit and the Commendation of Merit. She very much enjoyed helping other women in the services and would often invite many over to her apartment for dinner. As for the secret to her tremendous efficiency, May said she ran things in the Air Force as she would keep a house.

How would Geraldine Pratt May view the position of military women today? She would certainly be heartened by some of the changes such as increased career choices, but she would be saddened, too. Continued reports of sexual harassment and the number of jobs open only to men would undoubtedly remind her of the Vandenberg era of over 40 years ago.

Antonia Novello ─────────────

Antonia Novello is a doctor who knows what it is like to be a patient. Born with congenital megacolon (an abnormally large, malfunctioning colon), she was chronically ill as a child and required hospitalization for at least two weeks every summer. She was promised corrective surgery at age eight, but never received it because, she says, it was simply forgotten. Novello adds that some people have a knack for falling through the cracks, as she did. It was not until she was 18 that a cardiovascular surgeon agreed to attempt corrective surgery. Complications followed, however, requiring Novello to fly to the Mayo Clinic and remain there for two months, recovering and undergoing additional surgeries.

Novello emerged from her experience with great compassion for the sick. Her dream was to be a doctor to all the children in her village to ensure that no one would have to wait as long as she did for surgery. Over the years, Novello had become acquainted with many doctors, and she soon recognized the qualities that make a doctor great: kindness and caring. According to Novello, good doctors — and she had several — take the time to talk to their patients as people.

In her triumph over chronic illness, Novello also learned self-confidence and determination. After her second surgery, Novello had to wear adult diapers for six months, but, undaunted, she enrolled at the University of Puerto Rico. It was here that she earned a bachelor of science degree in premedical studies in 1965. Novello has shared her medical history to help people realize that illness does not prevent achievement; problems do not take away possibilities.

Still, Novello's dream of becoming a doctor seemed very ambitious. She was born Antonia Coello in Fajardo, Puerto Rico, in 1944 to middle-class parents. Novello's father died when she was eight and her mother, a school principal, married an electrician. Novello herself was fearful of rejection, so it was only after she was accepted that she told her mother she had applied to medical school.

Novello's mother was very supportive of her daughter, vowing that somehow she would fund money for her daughter's tuition.

Novello graduated from the University of Puerto Rico Medical School in 1970. During medical school she met Joseph Novello, a fellow physician and naval officer. They were married in 1970 and together moved to Ann Arbor, Michigan, where Antonia embarked upon a pediatrics residency at the University of Michigan and Joseph a psychiatry residency. She excelled during her residency, winning Intern of the Year in 1971.

Medical problems plagued Novello again, however, and she was hospitalized for kidney maladies in 1971. In addition, her favorite aunt, who had nursed Novello when she was younger, died of kidney failure. Now, as it had before, illness proved instrumental in Novello's career; after completing her residency in pediatrics she pursued subspecialty training in nephrology (the study of kidney diseases), first at the University of Michigan and then at Georgetown University Hospital.

Novello then went into private practice in Springfield, Virginia, but left after two years to pursue a career in the Navy. The captain who interviewed her was not welcoming, reiterating that the Navy needed good *men.* Little did he realize that he was turning down the future surgeon general of the United States. Novello was not to be deterred, however, so she went to the National Institutes of Health (NIH) and was accepted. Lieutenant Antonia Novello began active duty immediately. Novello soon ascended to the highest echelons of the NIH.

Novello found that she enjoyed the public health field very much and earned a master's degree in public health in 1981 from Johns Hopkins University in Baltimore. She then worked as a legislative fellow under U.S. Senator Orrin Hatch, who was then chairman of the Committee on Labor and Human Resources. She played an important role in the development of the National Organ Transplant Act of 1984, legislation which facilitates organ transplants for needy patients.

In 1986 Novello was named deputy director of the National Institute of Child and Health Development, one of the highest positions at the NIH. In this capacity Novello became involved in pediatric AIDS research and women's health issues. She felt she had reached her highest level of success, and planned to remain in this position until her retirement at age 52.

But a higher honor awaited Antonia Novello. On October 17, 1989, President George Bush nominated Novello to be the U.S. Surgeon General. On March 9, 1990, Dr. Antonia Novello was sworn in as the 14th surgeon general of the United States. She was the first woman, first Hispanic and first Puerto Rican to hold that position.

The little girl who wanted to be a doctor for the little children in her village had now become the "doctor for all Americans." As surgeon general, Dr. Novello's role was to bring the health problems of the nation to the attention of the Secretary of the Department of Health and Human Services and the assistant secretary of health, who then draft and enact public health policy. The surgeon general was also a public spokesperson on policy issues, issuing warnings about health hazards.

Novello held the rank of a three-star Vice-Admiral of the U.S. Navy while surgeon general and viewed her position as a developmental process, comparing it with the children in pediatrics who crawl before they walk and run. She took time to listen and to study before launching into major campaigns. Novello, like many in the Bush administration, opposed abortion. She herself was born with a congenital defect, therefore she believes everything should have a chance to live. This was one of the many issues she addressed.

Novello felt that her training as a pediatrician had prepared her to become surgeon general. She also believed her gender and minority status had gave her a better understanding of the issues she faced.

As a pediatrician, she was sensitive to the problems of the whole family. As a woman, she learned diplomacy and consideration for others. As an Hispanic, she understood that minority groups often have inadequate access to health care.

One of Novello's major campaigns as surgeon general targeted teenagers, a group she felt to be at risk. Her objectives included reducing the incidence of smoking, alcohol abuse and violence which have escalated in recent years. Another health problem Novello addressed was in the area of preventive medicine — prenatal care, vaccination of children, and injury prevention. These measures if properly carried out would reduce infant mortality greatly. Novello is also concerned with women's health issues. She always said she hoped that women would not hesitate to call and enlist her help in important concerns.

Dr. Antonia Novello's motto of good science and good sense, together with minimizing bureaucracy, became a potent combination which no doubt will continue to have a major impact on American public health policy.

Marie T. Rossi

During the Persian Gulf War, Major Marie T. Rossi was one of many women who served in the area. The night before the initial ground assault, a CNN reporter thrust a microphone at her, asking her how she felt about doing a man's job. Marie's response was clear: She felt that military women saw themselves as soldiers, that it was not an issue of gender, nor was it of greater or lesser value than what other soldiers around her were doing. Rossi further aroused the admiration and respect of the American people when she then told the CNN interviewer that she was ready to meet the challenge that her training had prepared her for — combat.

Born on January 3, 1959, Marie T. Rossi's leadership abilities were evident even when she was a child. It seemed natural for her to pursue U.S. Army ROTC training; she graduated as a second lieutenant in 1980. After a short stint as an artillery officer, Rossi found her true calling — flying helicopters. It was while flying Chinook helicopters in South Korea that she met her future husband, John "Andy" Cayton, a warrant officer who was also a helicopter pilot. Cayton would serve in Desert Storm too, but in a different unit.

Rossi, pilot and commander of B Company, 18th Army Aviation Brigade, did not flinch at the prospect of leading her squadron of Chinook helicopters into Iraq at the start of the war. Her commander did, though. He told her that male pilots were going to take the place of women because of the restriction against women in combat. When Marie Rossi countered by asking whether enlisted women on the crews were also going to lose their positions to men, he replied that they would not. Rossi told him emphatically that there was no reason the officers should be replaced. Her commander conceded that she was right.

Rossi's career in the military was a ground-breaking one. She became the first U.S. female helicopter pilot to fly into battle zones, carrying troops and supplies. Despite several hazardous flights into Iraq during Desert Storm, she flew skillfully and did not sustain any injuries.

Then tragedy struck and the entire United States mourned. On the night of March 1, 1991, the day after the cease-fire, Marie T. Rossi was killed when her Chinook crashed into an unlit tower during bad weather. Her death shocked the nation and brought into stark clarity the new roles women have assumed in the military. As warrant officer Ken Copley said, she was one of the most respected pilots he had ever known.

Tragically, Major Marie T. Rossi made us realize that whether it is a man or a woman who dies in battle the end result is that a human life has been lost. Whether that person is a father, brother, son or a mother, sister, or daughter, the loss is equally painful. Yet if women like Marie T. Rossi die answering our country's call the least we can do is to recognize their courage and selflessness without prejudice. Major Marie T. Rossi was a true patriot who will live on in the pages of U.S. history.

Deborah Sampson Gannett

Many women have proven that they can successfully endure the mental and physical hardships of battle. Throughout history there are many examples of women who enlisted in the military disguised as men, such as the courageous Deborah Sampson. In her autobiography *The Female Review,* published in 1797, Sampson wrote that she wanted to come to the aid of her fellow Americans in the War for Independence "or, to perish, a noble sacrifice, in the attempt." So she dressed as a man and enlisted in Captain George Webb's company of light infantry, 4th Massachusetts Regiment. She gave her name as Robert Shurtlieff. For this daring action, she may have been excommunicated by the First Baptist Church of Middleborough, the town where she lived as a child.

Because Deborah Sampson's officers and fellow soldiers believed her to be "just another soldier" she was not spared any of the grueling aspects of combat. No one was surprised by her quiet bravery and strength because, after all, she was a man. But, of course, she was not a man. Not a single soldier in Deborah Sampson's company minded having Robert Shurtlieff at his side.

Then what was the difference between Robert Shurtlieff and Deborah Sampson? The difference lay in the attitudes of her fellow soldiers and officers. They could accept Robert Shurtlieff as a comrade in arms but not Deborah Sampson, *even* if they were the same person.

Writing about herself in the third person as was the custom, Deborah Sampson recounts how once she was helping build "a Colonnade, or rather a Bowery, on West Point ... completed after about three weeks' fatigue. In this business, our heroic female often worked against the most robust and expert soldier: and had not the delicate texture of her frame been concealed, it would, doubtless, have been judged, that she was very unequally mated."

Deborah Sampson was born on December 17, 1760. There were six children in the family. Deborah's father had gone to sea and Deborah's mother learned some years later that he had died. Another source, however, states that he simply abandoned the family. Sampson's mother was poverty stricken and in ill health. When Sampson was five years old she was sent way from her home in Plymton, Massachusetts, to live with a Miss Fuller, a childless cousin of her mother's. Fuller turned out to be a very kind person who even gave young Deborah reading lessons. Sampson quickly learned the alphabet because she was very eager to understand what words meant. For three years she lived happily with Fuller.

Then tragedy again entered Sampson's young life. Kind, generous Miss Fuller grew very sick one day and three days later she was dead. Sampson's mother was still very ill and could barely care for herself. Sampson was forced to go to another strange house.

The minister of Middleborough, Benjamin Thomas took in Sampson, to live with him and his family. Deacon Thomas promised to provide her with a roof over her head, food, and clothes. Sampson, for her part, promised to work very hard, helping with chores and caring for the deacon's young children. For ten years she was a servant in the Thomas household.

Sampson was much too busy most days to spend time reading, her favorite pastime. She did teach the three oldest Thomas boys how to read. When the summer school opened in town, the boys were well-prepared. Young Deborah begged Deacon Thomas to let her attend school even a few days a month but she could not be spared. There was too much work to be done around the house. She remembers, "Wounding was the sight of others going to school, when she could not, because she could not be spared."

So at night, when all her work was done, Sampson pored over the schoolbooks of the Thomas children and kept a journal. On more than one occasion Deacon Thomas admonished, "I wish you wouldn't spend so much time in scrabbling over paper." Yet that was impossible for Deborah, whose autobiography reveals a lively, inquisitive mind.

Sampson was fascinated by nature. Sometimes she would wake up, when the grass was still cool with dew, and watch the sunrise from a nearby hill. Deborah Sampson wrote in her book:

> It has been a source of astonishment and mortification to her, that so many of her own, as well as of other sex, can dwell, with rapture on a romantic scene of love, a piece of painting or sculpture, and, perhaps, upon things of more trivial importance; and yet can walk in the stately and venerable grove, can gaze upon the beautifully variegated landscape, can look with indifference upon

the rose and tulip, or can tread on a bank of violets and primroses, without appearing to be affected with any peculiar sensations or emotions.

Deborah Sampson turned 18 in 1778. She said good-bye to the oldest Thomas boy as he went off to fight in the Revolutionary War. Sampson, too, said good-bye to the Thomas family. The Thomas children were all older now and someone was needed to teach the summer school in town because the war had taken all the men. Sampson's hard work had paid off.

Deborah Sampson had 20 students in her class and there were even some girls. Sampson was told to teach the girls only sewing, knitting, and how to read a little. But she remembered how she had longed to learn much more when she was a girl. So Sampson decided she would teach the girls exactly what she taught the boys. She did such a good job she was asked to return the next summer.

During the winter Sampson worked as a weaver. With the money she earned and the money she saved from selling the sheep Deacon Thomas had let her raise, Deborah Sampson decided to attempt something very daring. She was going to go home to her mother dressed like a man.

Sampson wove some cloth which she wrapped around her chest to make her look as flat-chested as a boy. She made a man's suit for her five feet seven inch frame and purchased a man's hat and shoes. Dressed up in her new clothes, she knocked on her mother's door. Opening the door her mother peered out but did not recognize her daughter. Maybe, just maybe, Sampson thought, others would think she was a man too.

When spring arrived, Deborah Sampson, dressed as a man, walked 35 miles to Billingham, Massachusetts, and she joined the Army on May 20, 1782, as a continental soldier.

For the first few weeks, Sampson lived in constant dread that someone would discover that she was really a woman. She was reluctant to speak in the beginning because she was unsure that she would be able to make her voice deep enough. Yet, the days passed and no one suspected. The other soldiers merely thought she was young — 15 perhaps — because she had no whiskers. Some Americans were only 16 when they enlisted. Most of her fellow soldiers called her Bobby. Other times they would tease her and call her "Blooming Boy," "Smock Face," or "Molly" because of her smooth face.

Deborah Sampson's first trial as a soldier was marching with 50 men to West Point, New York. The march lasted nearly two weeks, and was a grueling experience. In the evening the soldiers took baths in the Hudson River, but Sampson always took hers late at night. She slept, as all the soldiers did, in her clothes. She altered her army uniform so that it would fit better. Some soldiers saw how well Sampson could sew and grew slightly suspicious; she quickly explained that she had learned to sew as a boy because there were no girls in her family.

Deborah went on many marches and even in wintertime she says that she found herself "destitute of shoes, as were most of the soldiers . . . except raw hides, which they cut into straps and fastened about their feet. It was not uncommon to track them by the bleeding of their feet on the snow and ice."

Sampson was often hungry, too. She witnessed first-hand the pain and misery of war, seeing young people die who had so many more years to live. She watched men shot and heard them cry out the names of loved ones in their final agony. Danger was constant. Sampson once escaped a skirmish with two shots through her coat and one through her cap. She wrote in her book that when the two main armies got together in open field action

> The ground actually trembled for miles by the tremendous cannonade, which was incessantly maintained by boths sides day and night. . . . The nights exhibited scenes, to the highest degree, solemn and awfully sublime. Perpetual sheets of fire and smoke belched, as from a volcano, and towered to the clouds. And whilst the eye was dazzled at this, the ear was satiated and stunned by the tremendous explosion of artillery and the screaming of their shot.

Never did Deborah Sampson consider leaving the battlefield; she could have done so easily by slipping into her true identity. She did have ample opportunity, though, for as she describes: "One of her company having been severely chastised for stealing poultry, importuned her to desert with him and two others. But she not only disdainfully refused, but used all the eloquence, of which she was mistress, to dissuade them from so presumptive an attempt. . . ."

Knowing that her mother would be worried about her, Sampson wrote to her cryptically saying, "I am in a large, but well regulated family."

On one scouting mission during the winter, Deborah Sampson was riding with a few other soldiers to a cave containing food stolen by Tories to feed the British soldiers. Suddenly the Tories discovered the Yankee contingent. Swiftly the Americans mounted their horses, with the Tories following close behind. In the chase Deborah Sampson was shot. She wrote:

> She thought she felt something warmer than sweat run down her neck. Putting her hand to the place, she found the blood gashed from the left side of her head freely. She said nothing; as she thought it no time to tell of wounds, unless mortal. Coming to a stand, she dismounted, but had not the strength to walk, or stand alone. She found her boot on her right leg filled with blood; and in her thigh, just below her groin, she found the incision of a ball, whence it issued.

Sampson was taken to a hospital where a doctor bandaged her head. He asked her if she had any other injuries and she quickly shook her head no. She was terrified someone would discover her secret and she would be discharged from the Army because she was a woman. Before the doctor left the room she "requested the favor of more medicine than she needed for her head; and taking an opportunity, with a penknife and needle, she extracted the ball from her thigh; which, by that time, had doubtless come to its feeling." She then bandaged her bleeding leg that was bleeding profusely.

Most soldiers with such a wound would have been sent home, never to return to battle. But Sampson's only concern was discovery. For this reason, Sampson left the hospital before she was completely healed and the leg troubled her for the rest of her life.

Two weeks after suffering the wound Sampson was marching with her regiment again. A fellow soldier named Richard Snow was marching with Deborah Sampson when he dropped to the ground. He was ill and could not go a step further. Sampson volunteered to take Snow to a nearby farmhouse. She would catch up as soon as she was able. They were in Tory territory and danger abounded, and the regiment could not afford to wait for Richard Snow to get better. Sampson would have a chance to help Snow and also, she reasoned, give her leg some extra healing time.

The nearby farmhouse belonged to a man named Vantassel. He was not very welcoming but he allowed Deborah and the frail Snow to use his attic, which was freezing cold. Sampson strongly suspected that Vantassel was a Tory. She was right. Nightly he threw raucous parties for his Tory friends.

It was clear to Deborah Sampson that Richard Snow was dying. She pleaded with Vantassel to give the agonizing man at least a straw bed to sleep on. Vantassel refused. After ten days Richard Snow died. Deborah Sampson wrote: "It is not within my power to describe her melancholy distress in a dark garret with a corpse. A multitude of cats swarmed in the room; and it was with difficulty she disabled some with her cutlass, and kept the rest from tearing the body to pieces."

With the help of two others, Sampson was able to bury Snow. She then headed out and found her regiment. Accompanied by fellow soldiers under her command, Sampson surprised Vantassel and his Tory friends and they became prisoners of war.

In November 1782 Deborah Sampson traveled with her company to Fort Ticonderoga where she saw some action against the Indians. Robert Shurtlieff's commitment, dedication, and quiet bravery eventually came to the attention of a General Patterson (likely General Samuel Patterson of the Delaware militia) and he selected Sampson to be his personal orderly. It was a great honor.

In June Sampson traveled to Philadelphia on a very important mission. Angry soldiers had seized the State House and Congress was forced to move to Princeton, New Jersey. American soldiers were to be paid $6.67 a month but Congress did not have money to pay them. Most soldiers continued fighting even without pay but others refused.

Deborah Sampson arrived with 1,500 other soldiers to restore law and order. But in Philadelphia a dangerous fever was spreading. Many people fell ill and many of them died. Sampson came down with the fever, and was sent to the hospital. When she regained consciousness she overheard two men arguing over which of her clothes each was going to take because they thought Deborah Sampson was dead. Gathering every last ounce of strength she had, she made an attempt to speak so that the nurse on duty would realize that she was *not* dead. The nurse ran off to inform the doctor that patient Robert Shurtlieff was still alive.

But when Dr. Binney (Deborah Sampson refers to him as Dr. Bana) came to her bedside, Deborah had slipped back into a coma. Sampson's worst fear became a reality. The doctor examined her and learned her carefully guarded secret: "Robert Shurtlieff" was really 23-year-old Deborah Sampson.

The doctor might have asked himself *why* a woman would *want* to go to war and end up in an army hospital. For Deborah Sampson the answer would have been, simply, that she possessed the strength and soundness of mind to fight for America's freedom.

Dr. Binney concealed Deborah Sampson's secret. He even introduced Deborah to his family as the brave Continental soldier Robert Shurtlieff. Deborah writes that with Dr. Binney's daughters

> she had the happiness to recommend herself much to the esteem of his discreet and amiable daughters. And the Doctor was fond that so prominent a stripling should often gallant them into the city and country villages. The unruffled surface of a summer's sea was also often witness to their pastimes. This rare species of innocent recreations was, doubtless, peculiarly gratifying to the Doctor; as his mind could not be more at rest on his daughters' account.

When Sampson grew strong enough, she left Philadelphia. But before she left, Dr. Binney gave her a letter to give to General Patterson. Arriving at the camp the first days of October, she gave

General Patterson the doctor's letter and hurriedly left the room as General Patterson unfolded it. She had an idea what it might contain. An hour later General Patterson sent for her. When the general confronted her, Sampson told him the truth.

On October 23, 1783, Deborah Sampson was honorably discharged from the Army with an excellent record of service. Returning to Massachusetts she met Benjamin Gannett, a farmer from the town of Sharon. They fell in love and were married in April 1784. They had three children—a boy and two girls named Earl, Mary, and Patience. The Gannetts also adopted a little baby named Susanna. The baby's mother had died in childbirth and her father was unable to care for the baby by himself.

Sampson's leg from the war injury was causing her pain and she was unable to do much of the heavier farmwork. The farm was not prospering and the family needed money. So at 41 Sampson decided she would go out and obtain the money her family needed. Deborah Sampson then became the first woman lecturer in the history of the United States.

Many people had heard of the amazing story of soldier Robert Shurtlieff who was really a woman. The story had appeared in newspapers in Massachusetts and even in one New York newspaper. It made for exciting reading. Everyone was curious about Deborah Sampson and her life as a Continental soldier. Deborah Sampson gave her first talk in Sharon. She spoke about her Army days and put on her old uniform to do the manual of arms. She was a tremendous success.

In 1802 Sampson began in earnest to lecture about her Army experience. She traveled to Boston, Providence, and New York while Ben stayed home with the children and minded the farm. But after a year of lecturing, Deborah missed her family more and more and her leg was causing her considerable discomfort. She came home to stay.

In 1804 Paul Revere met Deborah Sampson for the first time. He had already heard of her bravery and daring as a soldier. Revere had formed a mental picture of Sampson as a tall, masculine-looking woman who was aggressive and possessed little compassion.

But when he met Deborah Sampson he wrote that she was gentle, quiet, well-educated and deserved better than to live in such poverty. Revere appealed to the Massachusetts authorities on her behalf. In 1805 Congress granted her a pension of $4.00 a month as a wounded veteran. In 1818 this sum was doubled.

On April 29, 1827, at the age of 76, Deborah Sampson died. Upon her death, Congress granted her husband a widow's pension.

Deborah Sampson was laid to rest in Sharon, Massachusetts. One part of the memorial for the war dead of Sharon is dedicated to Deborah Sampson Gannett, "revolutionary soldier." Deborah Sampson was revolutionary indeed. In her book she reflects soberly: "Custom, in many respects, rules us with despotic sway: And the person who greatly deviates from it, exposes himself to numberless dangers. An indelible stigma may doom him to infamy; though perhaps, his original design was to effect some useful and important event."

Flora Sandes

Throughout history, in times of great need and peril, women have fought in guerrilla warfare or in resistance movements. These are special situations and women were used only during desperate moments. No one denies that the women fighters were as successful as the men, but when the need for their services is at an end, women were expected to return quietly and uncomplainingly to their homes and resume their womanly function, once more deferring to the "superior" fighting and thinking skills of the men. Yet here and there women have refused to conform to the mold that society prescribed. This has been, in most cases, at tremendous personal cost.

Flora Sandes was born in 1876, the daughter of an English clergyman in Marlsford, Suffolk. She had five brothers and three sisters. Sandes' early days were genteel and innocent, a world of tennis and croquet, of ladies' circles and teas. When of sufficient age, she was sent to finishing school in Switzerland.

It is not known if Sandes' family approved of her decision to become a nurse, but her intention was to serve with St. John's Ambulance Unit attached to the Serbian Red Cross. Mabel Grovitch had journeyed to England to recruit nurses who were well trained, for there were few in Serbia. The small band of dedicated, idealistic nurses left Victoria Station in London and traveled to Brindisi, Italy, then to Salonika and on to Serbia with Sampson's contagious smile speaking of her hopes for the future.

The senior surgeon of the Serbian Army, Vladimir Georgeovitch, was not thrilled with the English nurses. He felt that women were not fit to serve in hospitals where the plague was claiming the lives of so many, servicemen and doctors alike.

Sandes had never been exposed to such appalling conditions as she found in the hospital: the food was inedible, no medical supplies were available. The nurses were given a small room, with dirty, rotten straw mattresses infested with bed bugs and fleas placed on the floor.

It took one look for Sandes to decide that what Serbia needed first were supplies for the wounded soldiers. She knew that it was hopeless to try to obtain local help. Even had she been able to raise the money, there simply were no medical supplies available. Sandes packed her bags and returned to England where her efforts received immediate attention and yielded the medicines and basic equipment so sorely needed. Through the Red Cross, Sandes raised £2000 in two weeks. In the United States another nurse gathered a vast sum. Laden with the generous gifts of two countries, Flora and her American friend, a Miss Simmonds, returned to Serbia. Of course Major Georgeovitch could not refuse such heaven-sent gifts, but this did nothing to allay his suspicions of female nurses. Indeed he found it difficult to believe that a female could be effective in surgery.

But the Serbian army was so understaffed that, swallowing his pride, Major Georgeovitch was compelled to ask Sandes and Simmonds to take over the operating room, where gangrenous limbs were removed all day long. Simmonds, who was trained in surgery, assured Sandes that she would do the amputating; Sandes need only apply the anesthesia. But before any operations were conducted, the two young ladies decided to scrub the room from top to bottom, something which had not been done in months, if ever.

Watching Simmonds, Sandes learned quickly and she, too, began to perform amputations. Overwork and the miserable living conditions made Sandes succumb to the on-going typhus epidemic. For three weeks she lay between life and death. Her will to live won, and shortly thereafter, with the coming of spring, the epidemic ended.

The tide of war was not favoring Serbia. All connections between Nish and Belgrade had been severed. Many a night after locking the door of her room (Sandes now had a tiny room in a hotel) she inspected and cleaned the small revolver which she kept by her all night. No one's safety could be guaranteed.

The British consul's well-meant efforts to keep Sandes safe were persistent; he continuously tried to persuade her to return home. Sandes hid herself in the field ambulance unit of the Second Serbian Regiment. The cover was effective and the consul gave up trying to convince her to return to the safety of her homeland.

The hospital where Sandes began to work was a large tent encircled by smaller ones, making what Sandes believed to be a "fairy ring" that would keep the patients safe from a sudden Bulgarian onrush. Predictably its magic powers did not last and on a dark and snowy night orders came to evacuate to a few miles north of Monastir. No trucks were available and so the wounded were loaded on carts. Sandes tried to communicate with the wounded and sick, smiling at them to give them courage while testing her growing knowledge of Serbian on her captive audience. Icy winds assailed them but Sandes's spirits were high; she felt she was contributing to the cause of the allies, a cause she believed in.

But she wondered if she could do more. Thus Sandes sought permission to join a fighting unit. When it was granted, she became a private in the Serbian army. She left the relative shelter and civilized surroundings of hospital tents and headed for the mountains.

The journey was a nightmare. On the way lay the unburied

remains of people, mostly very old and very young who are always the first to succumb to privations and exposure. Many soldiers perished in the attempt to cross high mountain passes blocked by snow, but Sandes trudged on until the weary and half-frozen troops reached a village.

Idyllic Lake Orchid was the setting of the last great battle of the war. With its placid waters at the foot of the Albanian mountains the lake seemed more suited for lovers and painters. The birds that played among the reeds sent their voices to the sky protesting the intrusion of humans, their bitter protests echoed potently by the cannon. But Sandes had to watch this battle from afar; the colonel had expressly forbidden her to go near the fighting lines.

Sandes was not pleased. Although the Serbian troops knew they could not win, they fought gallantly, awaiting the coming of the night to move. The king of Albania had agreed to let the Serbian troops cross his country, but the peasants, far removed from the court, were not friendly, and for the Serbians that trek to the frontier loomed long and hard along the dirt mountain trails.

The next day the Serbians found themselves nearly encircled by the enemy. In the heavy, frozen rain that seemed never-ending to Sandes, soldiers were deployed to keep the escape route open. The troops climbed on, always wondering if the Bulgars were waiting at the top to pounce upon them. The Serbians reached the summit ahead of the enemy, and Sandes settled down under cover of some rocks, a rifle in her hands, an uncomfortable feeling in her stomach. Of course, she had hunted in England, her aim was good, and she was familiar with firearms, but she had never dreamed of pointing a weapon at another human being. Night fell and with its coming renewed hope that the promised relief troops would arrive soon. But in the cold dawn, without new troops, Sandes followed her comrades to the warmth of the valley below.

Having proven her endurance, she was offered the opportunity of joining the Fourth Company, also as a private. Her dream of becoming part of a fighting unit had come true. Much later, when the weight of the years pressed upon her, Sandes looked back and judged this to have been one of her finest moments.

If Sandes expected excitement and glory, her first taste was of hardship. She camped in unhealthy, swampy fields, traveled in mud, climbed mountains, dug trenches and waited for the enemy to appear, dreading yet wishing for the moment of actual combat. The rains filled the trenches with water and the soldiers were always cold. Because of the lack of fuel, food had to be eaten cold, mostly canned beans and bread. Romantic and whimsical, the Serbian army had in its employ several violinists who played in the waiting hours and during lulls in fighting, filling Sandes with an unspoken nostalgia and sweet happiness. Sandes later remembered those violinists with a sense of unreality, a fairy-tale quality unreconcilable with the cruelty of war. The company was now en route to the coast. Years later, when she was bedridden and unable to sleep, Sandes thought back to those times when she slept as long as she could, fully dressed, with her helmet on, more crouching than sitting, in a muddy hole or in a snow drift.

Sandes had also fallen in love. It was an unspoken love, for conventions were rigid and the man she loved was a lieutenant. At the beginning Flora thought Lieutenant Janachko Jovitch was hostile and they had many arguments, each loath to concede to the other's point of view. Lieutenant Jovitch had been born in Belgrade. His father had died when Jovitch was very young, and he was raised by his mother, a school teacher who earned a meager living. Jovitch had to help his mother while still a child and he left school to work. An idealist, he had joined the army to help drive the Turks from the Balkans. Although Jovitch seemed in their campfire discussions opposed to almost everything Sandes represented, unbeknown to her, he had given Sandes his small meal allowance—a piece of bread—many times.

The company was nearing Durazzo, the most important port on the Albanian coast. Sandes felt sick and dizzy from exhaustion and from the stench of the dead horses along the road. The soldiers were too tired to bury the animals; only humans were interred. Yet there were advantages to being a woman, Sandes thought. As long as the company was in camp, she was given the privilege of occupying a small tent by herself.

Just as Sandes was beginning to feel comfortable as a soldier, she discovered how much she had to learn. For her lapse, she was severely reprimanded. Sandes was invited by an officer of another battalion to lunch. Of course she was aware that she needed the permission of the commander to leave camp, but when she could not find him, she went anyway. She had such a wonderful time that she remained for dinner as well. She was happy and tired, replete with good food, a rare occurrence, and slept like a baby. Early the next morning she was ordered to present herself to the commander. Sandes left his tent, her face aflame, knowing that she was the only one responsible for what she later termed her stupidity.

The next destination of the troops was the Greek island of Corfu. Bleak, rainy weather met them, there was no wood for fires, no hay to stuff mattresses, no supplies, and no hope. Even then Sandes would not give up. Expecting to obtain some supplies she went to the British Mission. The major who headed the Mission assured her that there was nothing he could do to help her company. Next Sandes went to the Serbian Headquarters where once again she was denied help. The French, in charge of food, were no more helpful.

Undaunted, Sandes made the rounds once more. Faced with a second denial, she could no longer stem the tide of words and tears. This was just as well, for the French colonel was moved at last to accede to her request. Sandes had not intended to cry; she was simply exhausted, frustrated, and, above all, mad. She could not face returning to the hungry company with no food or fuel. But now thanks to the "womanly behavior" of which she was so ashamed, she would go back with bully beef and bread. Tomorrow, the French colonel assured her, the Fourth Company would be put on the supply list.

With a triumphant smile, Sandes imagined the reception she would get back at camp. She was so resourceful that Lieutenant Jovitch was happy to accede to Sandes' request to work with the Serbian Relief Fund, the organization that administered the aid supplied by the British and the French. By this time, Sandes could speak Serbian; she had always been fluent in French and German. Sandes' hard work was rewarded with a promotion to sergeant.

Not long afterwards, the Second Regiment left Salonika. Their destination was the front and fighting. Sandes was ready. Her training had been extensive and disciplined. If the objective of the allies was to defeat the German and Austrian Empire, she was going to do her part to help.

Her Second Regiment fought its way through the mountains, hoping to reach Austria by way of Macedonia and Serbia to Belgrade, before crossing into Austria. Unfortunately, the army no longer had its previous strength. Of the 600,000 soldiers available at the beginning of the war, about 120,000 had survived. Life in the trenches and daily privations were made more bearable for Sandes by her love for Jovitch which was growing and strengthening.

The enemy artillery began shelling their camp and the Serbian troops were forced to move up the mountain, abandoning all their equipment except ammunition and knapsacks. Up and up they climbed in the total darkness of a moonless night, their path lit by exploding enemy grenades. Rain fell incessantly, and the cold wind buffeted the high peaks. Without natural, or artificial, protection, the soldiers shivered all night long, while the hot sun of midday was unbearable. The next morning the soldiers were on the run, dodging enemy fire, trying to keep in the protection of their own artillery. Bodies, enemy and friend alike, were strewn in their path. Sandes had seen death as a nurse, but not the torn bodies of friends that no one could bury, for they could not stop.

Weeks of fighting followed. By now it was impossible to deny that the resistance was futile. The Serbian army, weakened by the loss of men and supplies, would advance a few yards after a bitter fight, only to have to give way the next day to the enemy.

Sandes spent her days in a water-filled hole or behind rocks, shooting and dodging enemy fire. As the retreat continued, she saw her comrades falling dead beside her. As the troops retreated down the mountain, a major held Sandes back. Lieutenant Janachko Jovitch was dead, he told her, killed by an enemy bullet.

The next days were nearly intolerable. The image of Jovitch was constantly with her, along with the never ending discomfort, the freezing rain, the snow, and the Bulgar attack cry "Houra! Houra!"

Sandes was awakened by the dreaded battle cry, just as the Bulgars were charging. Quickly she grabbed her carbine and in compliance with the order, fixed her bayonet. She started forward with the others, falling in the deep snow, getting up, and charging anew, seeking protection behind rocks, only to charge again. Suddenly, she felt pushed to the ground by a force she could not resist. She could not see, she could not move. Someone was dragging her through the snow, her mind registered, before the pain made her lose consciousness.

When she awoke she realized that she had been severely wounded. Despite her pain, Sandes begged her comrades to leave her, for the thought that they could be captured because of her was unbearable. However, using the little cover available, two of her comrades pulled and dragged her, finally arriving at the ambulance tent where her wound was probed for shrapnel from the enemy grenade. There was no anesthesia, but Sandes gritted her teeth and endured. As soon as it was possible, she was transferred to the hospital in Salonika. While in the hospital the aide-de-camp of Crown Prince Alexander presented Sandes with the coveted Kara George Star and announced that she was promoted to sergeant-major.

News from the front was grim. Many of Sandes' friends had paid for the few successes with their lives. Impatient with herself, Sandes cut her convalescence short to join the Fourth Company. But the Company no longer existed; the 16 survivors were now in the First Company. Sandes joined the First Company at the Starovenski Redoubt.

The monotonous days stretched for a long one-and-a-half years; the troop slept in dugouts during the day, lying silent and vigilant in the trenches at night. There was little fighting.

The shrapnel inside Sandes' body moved and she had to return to the hospital, after trying to fight what she perceived as a weakness. The doctor refused to release her back to the front, so Sandes, thinking she could serve the cause better at home, returned to England and began a writing campaign to inform the public of the privations and endurance of the Serbian soldiers. Her writing was impassioned and it brought results. Supplies poured into the trenches, where Greek, British, French, Italian, and Serbian fought side by side.

When Sandes returned to the regiment, there was a different feeling in the air. The war had lasted four years and the Allies had not broken the German-Bulgar defense. Finally, the Bulgars capitulated. As Flora passed through the villages, she saw the suffering, the burnt-out houses, and the ruins of previously prosperous towns. There was no harvest and the domestic animals had long since been requisitioned by the enemy. Parents did not know if their children had survived, and children searched for their parents. Desolation was everywhere. The Austro-Germans were retreating but they inflicted heavy losses as they passed.

Sandes fell ill with a fever and chills. There was no help available in the hospital, and it was only days later that a veterinary surgeon treated her with some medicine he used for the animals. It worked, although Sandes never knew what was given to her, and as soon as she was well, Sandes returned to the hospital where she had received no treatment, and accused the doctor of doing nothing to help the patients. What could he do, he asked, when he had no medicines, no supplies, and who was she, anyway, to reprimand a captain? She threatened to make a report accusing him of incompetence and negligence. If she thought she was more competent than he was, said the doctor, she could run the hospital herself. And with that he left.

Sandes was frightened at her new responsibility, but being Flora Sandes she was not inactive for long. She asked the orderlies to help and together they scrubbed the hospital, installed clean beds donated by the women of the town in response to her appeal, and prepared clean food.

In 1918 the armistice was signed and World War I ended. Sandes could no longer fight in the trenches, but she would try, in the long and hard fight that she knew lay ahead, to make Jovitch's dream of freedom come true. She would never give up.

Sandes continued in the army. In 1919 she was commissioned a second lieutenant which, because she was a woman, required a special act of parliament. Shortly thereafter Sandes married a Russian émigré, Yurie Yudenitch. A sergeant under Sandes, he had been a colonel in the Russian army under the Tsar. Like many of his fellow countrymen, he had emigrated with the fall of the monarchy.

The old way of life was gone forever. Demarcation lines had changed as well, and Yudenitch knew that he would have to live out his life in exile. The couple lived in Paris and Belgrade, never becoming rich but living comfortably. Unable to escape to safety before the arrival of the Germans in World War II, Sandes was interned, though not for long, in a concentration camp. Her husband died in 1941, and she returned to England. She died in Suffolk in 1956.

By Sandes' own admission, she often thought of those days and nights spent on the battlefield, of her campfire conversations with Janachko, of the ever present danger, but also the elation, the comradeship that was shared by all fighting for the same cause. If she had indeed helped the cause she believed in, she was satisfied that she had done her duty.

Cheryl Stearns

Cheryl Stearns, one of the finest athletes in the world, knew from an early age that she wanted to jump out of planes. When she was only 17, she persuaded her mother to pay a $40 fee and sign a release form so that she could make her first jump.

Stearns was born in Albuquerque, New Mexico, on July 14, 1955, but was raised in Scottsdale, Arizona. She began taking flying lessons at age 17, thanks to a $3,000 loan from her mother. She then became a flight instructor while earning an Associate of Arts degree from Scottsdale Community College, where she was on a tennis scholarship. By 1974 she was ready to compete in her first national skydiving competition. She finished in ninth place, which fueled her desire to improve and become a champion.

She decided to search for a mentor and trainer. A friend told her about Gene Thacker, an ex-member of the Golden Knights (the U.S. Army's elite parachuting team) who now coached award-winning skydivers. Stearns says she wrote to Thacker that she wanted to be a world champion but had no money. She also added that she had a dog. Thacker wrote back telling her not to worry because he would not let either her or her dog starve.

Gene Thacker was very willing to undertake the job of training Stearns. He has said that what impressed him most about Stearns was that at age 19 she had two years of college, general job experience and had obtained a pilot's license with a commercial rating. She obviously possessed extraordinary initiative. Thacker says that Stearns has a driving need to be the best at whatever she undertakes.

Stearns arrived at Thacker's home in Raeford, North Carolina, with $50 and her dog. She began working and training immediately. Thacker constructed an apartment in his new hangar for her, and she worked by packing parachutes, working on airplanes, putting down concrete and flying an airplane for jumpers. Three times while flying, the plane ran out of gas and had to glide to a landing. Stearns, who calls the sky "upstairs," took it in stride saying that, after all, it was not like being on fire. She just lost altitude.

Stearns also honed her own skydiving skills, jumping six times a day, seven days a week. She entered the national skydiving competition in 1975 and won first place in accuracy, eleventh place in style, and seventh overall. For the accuracy competition, Stearns had to land on a four-inch target in the center of a sandbox of pea gravel. She had to be able to gauge wind directions, handle her parachute, and land in the pit.

The style competition is just as difficult as the accuracy competition. Each jumper must perform six turns and loops within the first 30 seconds of jumping. Once the 30 seconds are over, the jumper must open the parachute and concentrate on landing. Stearns says her strategy is to dig into the air with her hands and work against it. She compares dropping out of a plane to being on a beam in gymnastics. But as in gymnastics one can tumble in the air and one can fall.

It did not take long for the U.S. Army's Golden Knights, whose home is in Fort Bragg, North Carolina, to recognize Stearns' talent and invite her to join their ranks as the first woman member. In February of 1977 Stearns enlisted in the Army. She served two three-year tours with the Golden Knights, emerging as one of the team's foremost performers. The Golden Knights swept national and international awards; for her contributions Stearns was awarded three Meritorious Service medals and six Army Commendation medals. Stearns says that her experience with the Golden Knights afforded her the chance to make her dream of becoming a world champion come true. Comradery in the corps was superb.

When she was not competing with the Golden Knights, Stearns worked as a flight instructor at Fort Bragg. She also went on to earn a Bachelor of Science in Aeronautical Administration and a Master of Aeronautical Science degree (both magna cum laude) at Embry-Riddle University's Fort Bragg campus. In 1985 Stearns retired from the Army with the rank of sergeant.

Stearns holds more titles and world records than any other skydiver, man or woman. In 1978 she broke the world record for day and night accuracy, jumping from 2500 feet to land directly on a four-inch target 43 times during the day and 23 times during the night. In 1978 Stearns and her colleague Russel Fish also broke the men's and women's record for number of jumps performed during 24 hours. As Stearns explains they jumped from an altitude of 2000 feet. When she landed she had to run about 30 yards and put on her chute. Stearns and Fish completed the record number of 255 jumps in 24 hours.

Stearns enjoys performing for an audience. She once landed on Liberty Island with the American Flag and twice landed on the 50-yard line of the Fiesta Bowl — once to bring the coin for the toss and another time to bring the football. She has also had her share of scares. On one occasion both of her parachutes malfunctioned and she hit the earth at 40 mph. When she recovered from her injuries she immediately returned to jumping.

In 1991 Stearns' impressive achievements — 13 U.S. Women's Overall National Championships, 11 world titles, 30 world records, and multiple international military parachuting titles—earned her the recognition of the International Parachuting Committee. On October 10, 1991 Stearns was awarded the Leonardo da Vinci Diploma, a great honor and recognition of her life's work.

Since leaving the Army, Stearns has taught aerobatics, flown medical air evacuation for a heart surgeon, and performed as a pilot and jumper for Air Show America. She currently serves in the Army National Guard and is a pilot for U.S. Air, with over 8,000 hours of logged flight.

She still enjoys very much spending time "upstairs." She spends about 90 percent of her time flying. She admits that she feels more at home in the skies flying planes, or jumping out of them, than she does on the ground. Stearns still competes in the U.S. nationals, bringing home gold medals and earning a spot on the U.S. Parachute Team. She also trains every year at the Golden Knights annual winter training in Yuma, Arizona. Her teammates welcome her as an inspiration for men and women.

In 1991 almost 10 percent of the Golden Knights were women. Her accomplishments with the Golden Knights have become tangible evidence to many that women can capably fulfill military roles traditionally reserved for men. Stearns has broken down many stereotypes about women in the military.

Dorothy Stratton

Dorothy Stratton was the coordinator and first director of the Women's Reserve of the Coast Guard. She nicknamed the women SPARS, from the Coast Guard motto Semper Paratus, which means "Always Ready." She dropped the women's previous, much less flattering, nickname, "Warcogs."

Born in Brookfield, Missouri on March 24, 1899, Stratton grew up in Kansas and Missouri. She attended Ottawa University in Kansas, immersing herself in a variety of campus activities: the school newspaper, student council, and the basketball team. She even won the women's tennis championship in the Kansas Intercollegiate Athletic Conference.

After receiving her Bachelor of Arts degree in 1920, she taught high school in Renton, Washington. In 1923 she became vice-principal of the Sturges Junior High School in San Bernardino, California. The following year she advanced to dean and vice-principal of girls at the Senior High School in San Bernardino. During this time Dorothy Stratton also worked to complete her own education, earning a Master of Arts degree in psychology at the University of Chicago in 1924 and a Doctor of Philosophy degree in student personnel administration at Columbia University in 1932. Her doctoral dissertation, *Problems of Students in Graduate School*, was published in 1933, the same year Stratton became dean of women and associate professor of psychology at Purdue University.

At Purdue, Stratton made changes which improved the college experience of women. She created a career placement center for women and was instrumental in the construction of three women's dorms. Prior to her work, there had been no housing for women on the campus.

In 1940 Stratton was promoted to full professor. In keeping with her ideal of teaching college students about character, citizenship, and culture, Stratton co-wrote with Helen B. Schleman a book specifically directed to college students, *Your Best Foot Forward,* published in 1940. For this book, Stratton and Schleman had distributed a questionnaire to students from nine college campuses across the country and obtained opinions from student leaders from 59 campuses.

In June 1942, as World War II escalated, Stratton joined the selection board of the Women's Army Auxiliary Corps (WAAC), helping select the first WAAC personnel to go to Des Moines to train in the Navy Women's Reserve (WAVES). Because it was a new career field for women and it was important to her that women give a good showing of themselves during the war effort and after, Stratton then decided to enlist in the WAVES herself. Lieutenant Stratton was in the first class of the Naval Training School at Smith College. She later became commanding officer at the Training Center for Radio Operators at Madison, Wisconsin.

In November 1942, she was assigned to the office of the commandant of the Coast Guard, where she helped formulate plans and policies for a Coast Guard women's reserve. The corps was authorized by Congress on November 23 and Stratton, now a lieutenant commander, was sworn in as director of the Women's Reserve of the U.S. Coast Guard.

During her years as director, Stratton said that she had never worked so hard and liked it so much. She rose to the rank of captain and supervised thousands of women who were ready and willing to fill demanding jobs so that men could go to sea. The SPARS worked in a variety of capacities, such as stenographers, pharmacy assistants, clerical workers, radio experts, photographers and more. Stratton sought women who would give every ounce of their energy to the arduous task of winning the war.

Stratton left her position as SPARS director in 1946, joining the Federal Retraining and Reemployment Administration. In this capacity she helped communities re-integrate women veterans after the war.

Stratton then turned her attention to a variety of other causes. She became director of personnel for the International Monetary Fund in Washington, D.C., from 1947 to 1950. In 1950 she became executive director of the Girl Scouts in America, a position she held until 1960. She also concerned herself with the physically challenged, serving in 1962 on the President's Commission on the Employment of the Handicapped. Additionally she worked for the Department of Health, Education, and Welfare as a consultant on vocational rehabilitation.

There are some people who live their lives so fully and give so much to others they deserve to live more than one lifetime. Dorothy Stratton was such a person. She broke important ground and helped gain respect for women in the military.

Ruth Cheney Streeter ——————————

Ruth Cheney Streeter, an outstanding Marine Corps officer, liked to joke that she entered the Marines because it was about the only service in the military that one of her family was not in. Two of her brothers had served in World War I; Charles Cheney spent 20 months overseas in the U.S. Army Engineers, and William Cheney had flown as a pilot in the Army Air Corps. Three of Streeter's four children also entered the armed forces, two in the Navy and one in the Army.

Born in Brookline, Massachusetts, on October 2, 1895, Streeter attended Boston schools and then studied at Bryn Mawr College from 1914 to 1916. On June 23, 1917, she married Thomas Streeter, a lawyer and businessman who acted as chief of the external relations bureau of Division of Purchase, Storage and Traffic of the U.S. War Department during World War I.

After their marriage, the Streeters lived in Morristown, New Jersey, where Streeter devoted herself to a multitude of civic activities. In addition to becoming involved in the Bryn Mawr Alumnae Association, Streeter was active in health and welfare projects such as the New Jersey State Relief Council, the New Jersey Commission of Inter-State Cooperation and the New Jersey Board of Children's Guards. With the advent of World War II, Streeter served as chairperson of the Fort Dix Citizens's Committee for Army and Navy, a group devoted to providing comforts for the men stationed at Fort Dix.

Streeter soon became further involved in aviation and in the war effort. She earned private and commercial pilot's licenses and was made an honorary pilot of the 126th Squadron of the Army Air Force. She also served on the Civil Air Patrol, on the North Jersey squadron of the New Jersey Civil Air Defense Services, and on New Jersey's Defense Council's Committee on Aviation.

On February 12, 1943, the Marine Corps enlisted the aid of 19,000 women reservists and appointed Streeter as director of the Marine Corps Women's Reserve with the rank of major. Nineteen

Women Accepted for Voluntary Emergency Service (WAVES), officers agreed to transfer to the Marine Corps to aid Streeter in her new position. Streeter accepted the post willingly, saying that no American could possibly refuse the Marines. Major Streeter insisted that the women not be referred to as "Marinettes" as they had been in World War I; instead, they would simply be called "Marines." The women's duty was to release male Marines from their jobs in the United States so that they could serve overseas and in combat. As already mentioned in this book, men in all the services, resented women replacing them in jobs that had been considered exclusively male. Too, they often did not want to leave their safe, Stateside assignments and the women became the obvious targets of their misplaced resentment. The women served as accountants, mechanics, cryptographers, draftspeople, aerographers, electricians, telegraphers and in a host of other positions. A Marine Women's Band, the first to be authorized by the Corps, replaced the previous all-male band. The new band took over such activities as parades, concerts and reviews.

Many of the rules of the Marine Corps Women's Reserve (MCWR) were different than the rules governing women Marines today. For example, both married and unmarried women could enlist, but if a married woman had children under the age of 18, she would not be eligible. If a woman was married to a Marine, she could not join the MCWR, but it was acceptable for a woman to marry a Marine after completing her training. Women were also not allowed to serve outside the continental United States on ships. Major Streeter, who was promoted to lieutenant colonel in November of 1943, was a strong proponent of women being permitted to serve overseas. She would have volunteered for such duty herself, insisting that she wanted to be where the most action was.

In 1945 Streeter received a promotion to colonel. She retired that same year, but continued her involvement in many civic and political activities. She served as a delegate to the New Jersey Constitutional Convention in 1947 and as Republican presidential elector in 1960. Together with her mother, Streeter also continued to sponsor an award to be given to an Army Air Corps member for acts of courage or selflessness. The award was in memory of her brother, William Cheney, who was killed during World War I in an air collision over Italy.

Streeter died in Morristown, New Jersey, in 1990. She had greatly helped shape and pave the way for women's involvement in the Marines. She also saw the fulfillment of one of her greatest hopes — that women would serve as pilots for the U.S. Marines.

Wilma Vaught

Approximately 56,800 U.S. troops died in the Vietnam War, including about 46,400 in combat. It is estimated that 303,700 Americans were wounded and about 2500 were missing. When we think of the Americans who died, lost limbs, or even left behind a precious thing called idealism in Vietnam, we rarely think of our American women.

However, many military women distinguished themselves during the Vietnam conflict. Once in Vietnam, they refused to return to the safety of their homes in the States. According to Major General Jeanne M. Holm, the courage and dedication of American military women under enemy fire should have closed the mouths of skeptics forever, particularly their performance during the Tet offensive. When attacks began, the Army decided to relocate the nurses to a safer area. The women refused. They had come to Vietnam to do a job and that is what they were going to do. And as it turned out, they did it extremely well. Not even two percent of those wounded in the Vietnam War died because of their battle injuries. This is an extraordinary statistic.

Brigadier General Wilma Vaught USAF (Retired) is a Vietnam veteran who has vowed to bring peace to all American women veterans. She wants to grant them, finally, the recognition they richly deserve and make Americans see the important, even crucial, roles in American military history women have filled, unclouded by prejudice.

General Vaught is the President of the Board of Directors of the Women in Military Service for America Memorial Foundation, Inc. This enormous and long-awaited project is the first large-scale national memorial to honor all women veterans and one of the first memorials to honor living veterans. Remembering those who should not be forgotten is General Vaught's objective; over two million women have served in the military since the Revolutionary War. The memorial comprises ten lighted glass prisms and a huge computer bank. Photos, memories, and war narratives are all stored in this bank.

General Vaught was born on March 15, 1930, to Willard L. and Margaret J. (Pierce) Vaught in Pontiac, Michigan. She received her Bachelor of Science degree from the University of Illinois, Champaign-Urbana in 1952. In 1983 she was awarded the Distinguished Alumni Achievement Award by the University of Illinois. Her Master of Business Administration degree she received from the University of Alabama in Tuscaloosa in 1968, and an Honorary Doctorate of Public Affairs from Columbia College, S.C., in 1991.

General Vaught is the recipient of countless military decorations and awards, including a Vietnam Service Medal with four service stars, Republic of Vietnam Gallantry Cross with palm and Republic of Vietnam Campaign Medal. General Vaught was also the first woman to deploy with a Strategic Air Command bombardment wing on an operational deployment, 1966–67.

One of the most decorated military women in U.S. history, General Vaught was the first Air Force woman to graduate from the Industrial College of the Armed Forces, Fort Lesley J. McNair in Washington, D.C. She is also the first and only woman granted promotion to brigadier general in the comptroller career field. In a military capacity General Vaught has traveled widely. Today, among other activities, General Vaught is often a guest on radio shows and television programs, divulging the truth about our brave military women.

Women in Military Service

Aethelflaed

A Saxon queen whose reputation as a military strategist persists to this day, Aethelflaed was the daughter of King Alfred. She married Ethelred, ruler of West Mercia, and presided with him over their kingdoms. When Ethelred died in 911 Aethelflaed continued to reign as Lady of the Mercians. Aethelflaed's military prowess soon emerged. She sent armies to aid her brother, Edward, the King of Wessex, in defeating the Vikings in eastern England. She also established camps and built fortresses such as Warwick and Stafford, which then became major commercial centers. She challenged the Danes in 917 and gained control of Derby and Leicester. She then took over Northumbria and parts of Wales. At the time of her death in 918 she was probably in the midst of further military campaigns in the north. Her brother Edward succeeded her.

Valérie André

A graduate of the Faculty of Medicine in Paris in 1948, André served in Vietnam as chief of medicine of a woman's infirmary and later as a neurosurgery assistant at a military hospital. In 1950 she received a commission as a helicopter pilot, flying some 150 medical rescues in the heat of battle. She was decorated nine times, receiving among other awards the Legion d'Honneur, Croix de Guerre and U.S. Legion of Merit.

André also served in the Algiers campaign as medical chief of a helicopter squadron, earning a colonelcy in 1970. She later became medical technical adviser to the aerial transports commander and subsequently chief of medical service. For her outstanding work she was promoted to general, the first French woman to hold this rank.

Artemisia II

When Artemisia's husband King Mausolus, ruler of Caria (Asia Minor) died in 352 B.C., she became queen. The people of

Rhodes felt a woman would be a weak ruler and planned to free themselves from Caria's control. When the Rhodesians sailed to Caria, Artemisia told her citizens to feign surrender. The Rhodesians thinking themselves victorious, began to destroy the city. They were held back, however, by soldiers hiding in the city walls. Meanwhile, other Carians set sail from a man-made channel connected to a hidden harbor and seized the Rhodesians' ships. They then adorned the ships with victory laurels and set sail to Rhodes, where they were welcomed by the citizens. The Rhodesians discovered too late that the ships contained Carians, not Rhodesian heroes. The Carians promptly took control of Rhodes. Artemisia erected two monuments in Rhodes to commemorate her victory.

Jacqueline Auriol

Auriol began flying as a hobby and by 1950 had become a military pilot for France. She later became at Brétigny the world's first woman test pilot. Auriol was also very interested in jets. In 1951, flying one of the first DeHavilland DH100 Vampires, she broke Jacqueline Cochran's speed record, attaining 507 miles per hour. She received the Legion d'Honneur and the American Harmon Trophy. Other records awaited her; she was one of the first to break the sound barrier, one of the first to fly the Concorde, and held the women's world speed record five times between 1951 and 1964.

Lakshmi Bai

Born in 1835 in Jhansi, India, Bai lost her mother when she was young and was then raised in an almost all-male household, where she became an expert in martial arts and horseback riding. She later married the Raja of Jhansi. When he died, with an heir, the British seized Jhansi and refused to recognize the heir. During the Indian mutiny in 1857, 22-year-old Bai joined in the battle against Britain, fighting side-by-side with her male counterparts. She was felled by a British soldier but lived in her people's memory as an Indian nationalist hero. During India's independence movement in the twentieth century, she was held up as an ideal of Indian patriotism.

Barbara Bell

Bell graduated at the top of her predominantly male class at one of the Navy's top jet schools, Patuxent River Naval Air Station in Maryland. In fact, her abilities were so outstanding that she was asked to return as an instructor, thus becoming the first woman to teach at the elite jet school. She later became the first woman to qualify as an F-14 radio intercept officer. Her goal, however, was to join an F-14 squadron aboard a carrier at sea, something the law at that time did not permit. Under current law, women are now training for such activities.

Gertrudis Bocanegra

Gertrudis Bocanegra, a Mexican freedom fighter born in 1765, organized an underground army of women during the Mexican War of Independence in 1810. The government arrested her, tortured her and killed her in 1817 by public execution as a warning to other patriots.

Maruya Bochkareva

Daughter of a penniless serf, Bochkareva, born in 1889, was sent to work at age eight. In 1914, after escaping her husband's attempt to murder her, she immersed herself in patriotism and the military. She became a soldier and received many decorations for bravery, most notably for rescuing wounded soldiers in the midst of machine-gun fire. In 1917, she proposed a "Women's Battalion of Death." Many women enlisted and Maruya Bochkareva received much publicity and praise from other feminists. Meanwhile, other women started to organize similar battalions, and, together with Bochkareva's, fought in July 1917. In 1918 the Bolshevik government sentenced Maruya Bochkareva to death, but she escaped to the United States.

Linda Bray

Captain Linda Bray was one of 770 military women sent to Panama for Operation Just Cause. When in December 1989 she led 30 soldiers of the 980th Military Police Company to seize a kennel for attack dogs of the Panamanian Defense Force, what was supposed to be a routine undertaking became a three-hour-long infantry-type battle. Captain Bray and her troops emerged victorious from the firefight. Although the captain did not lend the incident any particular significance, it became, according to sociologist Charles Moskos, a shot that was heard around the world, especially in the Pentagon.

The media exploded with stories about Captain Bray and controversy raged over the issue of women in combat. Unfortunately, many male soldiers' prejudice against women prompted them to send Captain Bray many furious and even obscene letters, which so affected her that she resigned from the Army. Still, public interest in the role of women in military combat did not abate, and would again be fueled during the Persian Gulf War.

Lucy Brewer

Pretending to be a man during the War of 1812, Lucy Brewer saw action as a Marine for three years aboard the USS *Constitution*. The Marine Corps later recognized Lucy Brewer, a.k.a. George Baker, as the first woman Marine.

Kit Cavanaugh

Born in Dublin in 1667 to wealthy parents, Kit Cavanaugh married Richard Welsh, a servant. In 1692 Welsh was drafted into the Army and in 1693 Kit Cavanaugh, masquerading as a man, joined the Army in order to find him. She saw action in Holland against the French and then joined her husband's cavalry regiment, the Scots Greys, where she participated in the battles of 1702 and 1703. After being wounded at Ramillies, her disguise was uncovered but she stayed on with the Dragoons as a cook. In 1712, Cavanaugh moved to England and became an innkeeper. She died at Chelsea Hospital in 1739 and was buried with full military honors.

Mary E. Clarke

Major General Mary E. Clarke became the last director of the Women's Army Corps (WAC) on August 1, 1975. By 1978, the WAC was abolished, eliminating the separate services for men and women in the military. Afterwards women officers slowly started to command large numbers of men, whereas before women officers had usually commanded only women. Major General Clarke was one of the leaders in this movement, taking command in 1978 of Fort McClellan, Alabama, the site of the Army's military police and chemical warfare schools, as well as the site for co-ed basic training.

The Army's first two-star women general, Clarke fought throughout her career for the Army to accept women as a vital part of their force. She asserts that the performance of women soldiers is far too important to go back to an exclusively male fighting force with only a handful of women.

Margaret Cochran Corbin

Margaret Corbin, born in 1751, was raised by relatives after her parents were killed during an Indian raid when she was five. She married John Corbin in 1772 and accompanied him when he went east to fight in the American Revolution.

On November 16, 1776, Margaret Corbin's husband was killed near Fort Washington, New York, by Hessians. Corbin, who had been watching her husband, immediately took his gun and fought in his place. She was badly wounded in the battle. She managed, though, to travel to Philadelphia, where the Continental Congress granted her a lifetime soldier's half-pay pension. From that time onward she was included on all military rolls.

Paula Coughlin

Lieutenant Paula Coughlin graduated from Old Dominion University and received her commission in the United States Navy in 1984. Since that date she has enjoyed an exemplary military career, having been designated an unrestricted naval aviator in 1987. Lieutenant Coughlin has been awarded one Navy Commendation Medal, two Navy Achievement Medals, three Meritorious Unit Commendations, the Armed Services Defense Medal and two sea service ribbons. Unfortunately, it is not such a stellar service record which has brought Lieutenant Coughlin into the military limelight.

Upon entering a Las Vegas hotel hallway during a convention of the Tailhook Association, a group promoting naval aviation, she was subjected to both verbal and physical harassment by her fellow officers. When she reported the assault to her commanding officer no action was taken to punish the guilty. Instead of letting the matter go uncorrected, Lieutenant Coughlin decided to go public with the facts about sexual harassment and the abuse in the Navy. Her courageous decision led to congressional hearings, the resignation of the Secretary of the Navy, the early retirement of Admiral Frank Kelso, and an intense Pentagon investigation. Lieutenant Coughlin's courage and unwillingness to tolerate sexual abuse have wrought an awareness of the problem and contributed to changing the attitudes of men toward their female colleagues.

Sue Dauser

Captain Dauser joined the Navy in September 1917 and served as a nurse in Scotland during World War I. In 1939 she became superintendent of the Navy Nurse Corps, organizing and directing the corps throughout World War II. During her tenure she argued strongly that nurses should receive rank and privileges equal to that of male officers.

Jane Delano

A trained nurse, Jane Delano, born in 1862, recognized a need for nurses to be organized so that their corps could be easily mobilized during war or disaster. She therefore became chairperson of the National Committee on Red Cross Nursing Services in 1909, which brought the organizational structure of the Red Cross to the nursing profession. In the same year she was elected president of the Nurses' Associated Alumnae (later the American Nurses' Association) and selected superintendent of the Army Nurse Corps. Under her direction 8,000 nurses were mobilized at the start of World War I and about 20,000 more were mobilized for duty overseas. In 1918 she created and organized the Department of Nursing within the Red Cross.

Alene B. Duerk

Rear Admiral Alene Duerk, born in 1920, joined the Navy in 1943 and was appointed head of the Navy Nurse Corps in 1970. In 1972 she was promoted to rear admiral, thereby becoming the first woman to attain flag rank in the U.S. Navy.

Sarah Emma Evelyn Edmonds

When the Civil War broke out, Sarah Edmonds, born in 1841, enlisted as a man under the name Frank Thompson. She fought for the Union in the battles of Blackburn's Ford, the first Bull Run and in the Peninsular Campaign of 1862. She also served as an aide to Col. Orlando Poe at Fredericksburg on December 13, 1862. Edmonds volunteered on several occasions to "disguise" herself as a woman in order to infiltrate Confederate lines and obtain military secrets. In April of 1863 she deserted for unknown reasons. She later attained a veteran's pension, and, shortly before her death in Texas in 1898, became the only woman mustered into the Grand Army of the Republic as a regular member.

Rani Gaidinliu

Born in India to poor parents, Rani Gaidinliu became a freedom fighter at age 13. In 1931, at age 16, she became a leader of the Nagas and organized a band of guerrilla warriors to fight against the British. After much bloodshed Rani Gaidinliu and her guerrillas were defeated. She was sentenced to life imprisonment and anguished in jail for 14 years until India gained independence. Nehru released Rani Gaidinliu in 1947.

Juliane Gallina

Gallina made military history when she was the first woman selected to be the U.S. Naval Academy's brigade commander. In the fall of 1991 Gallina assumed responsibility for the 4,300 midshipmen under her, supervising their military activities and acting as student liaison for top academy officials. The academy opened in 1845 and first admitted women in 1976, although women still constitute less than 10 percent of the midshipmen. Gallina was told that she was not picked because she was a woman but rather because they thought she was the best one. Gallina, an English honors major with minors in French and Spanish, also participated in crew and lacrosse, was editor of the literary journal *Labyrinth Magazine,* and vice president of the Women's Professional Association.

Mary Hallaren

Colonel Hallaren was the first woman to receive an officer's commission in the U.S. Regular Army, under the Women's Armed Services Integration Act of June 1948.

Anne May Hays

On June 11, 1970, Anne Mae Hays, along with Elizabeth P. Hoisington, became the first woman general in U.S. history. Chief of the Army Nurse Corps, Hays had served for 28 years, spanning three wars. At the time of her promotion she was organizing approximately 5,000 military nurses to care for Vietnam War soldiers.

Jeanne M. Holm

When Major General Jeanne M. Holm retired from the Air Force after 38 years of service, she was the highest ranking woman ever to serve in the armed forces of the United States.

Jeanne Holm, author, consultant, and government official, was born in Portland, Oregon, on June 23, 1921. She enlisted in the Army as a truck driver, dedicating much of her exemplary career to obtaining recognition for the role of women in the military. She was commissioned second lieutenant in the United States Army in 1943. Holm's book *Women in the Military: An Unfinished Revolution* provides a detailed history of women in the military. Throughout her career Holm steadfastly battled discriminatory policies against women. She insists that the service should find the best person for each job, whether male or female. According to Holm, this is viewed by many as an experiment in sociology and not as what it is—the utilization of resources that lead to a better defense of the United States. Through her many lectures, her advisory posts, the decorations she has been awarded (Distinguished Service Medal with oak leaf cluster, Legion of Merit, medal for Human Action, National

Defense Service Medal with Bronze Star) and all her other honors Major General Holm USAF (Retired) is a model for women going into the armed services.

Mu-ian Hua

No actual records exist of Hua, but she is immortalized in Chinese folksongs and legends. She probably lived during the reign of the Tartar Wei dynasty (386–577). Legend holds that when Hua's ailing father was conscripted to fight for the government, Hua served in his stead, disguised as a man. During her 12 years of battle, she distinguished herself with her bravery, leadership, and patriotism.

Amy Johnson

In May 1930, after logging only 50 hours of flying, Amy Johnson, born in 1903, converted a De Havilland Moth into a monoplane and became the first woman to make a solo flight from London to Australia, taking 17 days. An overnight sensation, she lectured and wrote for newspapers, all the while making solo flights from London to India and on to Tokyo and back. She also became the first woman to fly the length of the Atlantic from east to west.

At the onset of World War II, Amy Johnson aided the United Kingdom in the war effort by joining the Women's Auxiliary Air Force, transporting planes and dispatches throughout England. During a flight in bad weather her plane went down over the Thames Estuary and she was never seen again.

Beverly Kelley

At the age of 26, Coast Guard Lieutenant Beverly Kelley became the first woman to command a U.S. military vessel. A graduate of the University of Miami and the Coast Guard Officers' Candidate School at Yorktown, Virginia, she assumed control of the 14 male crew members aboard the Coast Guard cutter Cape Newagen in April of 1979. Her duties included search missions, antipollution patrols and law enforcement in the seas around Maui, Lanai, and Molokai.

Lydia Litvak

The Soviets allowed women to fly military aircraft and engage in combat during World War II. There were three all-female air regiments during the war, and all three saw action. Junior Lieutenant Lydia Litvak was part of the fighter regiment which made 4,419 combat missions and engaged in 125 air battles, defeating 38 enemy aircraft and damaging 42 others. Lydia Litvak and her fellow pilots were described as clear-headed, courageous, and resourceful. After Litvak shot down a German ace, he would not believe that she, a 23-year-old woman, could have been the attacker—until she described their dogfight in perfect detail.

Manto Mavrogenous

A member of a distinguished and wealthy Greek family, Manto Mavrogenous aided Greece in its revolution against the Turks. She purchased and maintained ships to prevent piracy near the Greek islands. She also organized a band of guerrilla fighters, whom she equipped at her own expense, and led them, often successfully, into battle against the Turks in the Peloponnese. Mavrogenous then poured the remainder of her wealth into maintaining the official Greek army. She was promoted to lieutenant-general for her efforts. Mavrogenous also wrote personal letters to women in England and France to procure sympathy and financial support for the Greeks.

Once Greece achieved independence, political controversy raged and Mavrogenous was forced to live in isolation, barely eking out an existence on a small pension. Although she received no recognition when she died in 1848, she is immortalized in Greek poems, folklore, and portraits.

Joice Mugari Nhongo

Born in 1955, Joice Mugari, who would become a legendary guerrilla fighter, ran away from home at a young age to become one of the "boys" in the bush. At 18 she was a freedom fighter and by age 21 she was leader of Chimoio, the largest guerrilla camp in Mozambique. She then married Rex Nhongo, another freedom fighter who shared her ideals.

Joice Mugari Nhongo's expert guerrilla skills soon earned her the nickname "Teurai Ropa" ("Spill-blood") Nhongo. She was wanted by the Rhodesian government, which in 1978 attacked Chimoio. Nhongo, though pregnant, fought alongside her comrades and gave birth two days after battle. She then sent her daughter to live in safety with friends in Zambia. Nhongo did not see her daughter until two years later, when Zimbabwe was created. Since then, Nhongo has held various government positions, including Minister of Youth, Sport, and Recreation, and Minister of Community Development of Women's Affairs.

Florence Nightingale

Florence Nightingale, born in 1820, revolutionized military nursing and health administration. Her deep concern for others was fostered as a child when she and her mother would visit the sick and poor. When Nightingale turned 24 she used personal funds to run the Institution for Sick Gentlewomen in London. This first administrative experience would serve her in good stead in her future endeavors.

In 1854 Nightingale volunteered for service in the Crimean War after having read of the atrocious conditions there. The secretary of war asked Nightingale to head a party of nurses in battling the filthy and germ-ridden state of the British Army's medical organization. She did so with astonishing results. Within just a few months she reduced the death rate from 42 percent to 2.2 percent.

The "Lady with the Lamp," as Nightingale was dubbed by British soldiers, returned to England a heroine. The British public raised £44,000 for Nightingale, enabling her to endow the Nightingale School of Nursing. The success of this school, along with her radical reform of the British Army Medical Corps made her an influential administrator as well as the first woman appointed to the Order of Merit by Queen Victoria.

Jacqueline Parker

Parker is a pilot who has never met a plane she did not like. In 1988 Captain Parker became the Air Force's first female test pilot. She says that while she enjoys flying the F-4, the A-7 attack fighter is her favorite plane.

Teresa Marné Peterson

Lieutenant Colonel Peterson became one of the first women pilots in the U.S. Air Force. Her duties included flying C-141 cargo planes and training pilots to fly high-performance jets. She also became the first woman commander of an Air Force flying training squadron in 1990.

Emilija Plater

During the early nineteenth century, when she was still a young girl, Emilija Plater felt Lithuania should be free from Russia, which had ruled it since 1795. Plater prepared herself for confrontation by studying military subjects and weaponry. She organized several insurgent bands, fighting the Russians at Daugaupils, Ukmerge, and Vilnius. When the insurgents were finally organized into proper military units, Plater became a company commander with the rank of captain. In a battle at Siaulenai, Plater's unit was routed by the Russians; her troops then entered Russia and laid down their arms. Plater refused to admit defeat, so pretending to be a peasant woman, she set off to Poland to join in the fighting there. She died en route at Justinava in 1831.

Melissa Rathburn-Nealy

At 20 years of age, Melissa Rathburn-Nealy became the first U.S. enlisted woman to become a prisoner of war, and the first U.S. female military POW since World War I. An Army truck driver, she joined her unit in Saudi Arabia in October 1991, while the Gulf War raged. She was frightened but did not turn away from her conviction that women should be in combat. She therefore refused to stay behind a desk and instead drove 24-wheel trucks that transported tanks. On January 30, 1991, she and her partner were captured by Iraqi troops. Rathburn-Nealy sustained a bullet wound and shrapnel in her arm and was taken to Basra and then to Baghdad. Although frightened by exploding bombs nearby, Rathburn-Nealy assured her parents during a phone call that her captors were beautiful people who had taken good care of her. Rathburn-Nealy returned to the United States in the first prisoner release, where she was greeted by General Norman Schwarzkopf.

Mary Read

As a child growing up in England in the late seventeenth century, Mary Read pretended to be a boy in order to receive an inheritance from her grandmother. Read then continued her disguise, working first as a servant at an inn, then as a footboy to a French nobleman, then as "powder-monkey" on a warship. After about six years she deserted the ship and joined an infantry unit in Flanders, where she saw action in many battles against the French. Read then became a member of the Light Dragoon cavalry. In the course of duty she fell in love with a Flemish trooper and revealed her disguise to him. They were soon married and, with money from their astounded fellow soldiers, left the army to open a tavern in Brabant.

Larissa Mikhailovna Reisner

Shortly after entering the University of St. Petersburg in 1913, Reisner embraced communism. She published an anti-war magazine, *Rudin,* from 1915 to 1916 and then wrote for Gorky's journal *Chronicle.* In 1918 she put down the pen and picked up the sword, fighting as a Bolshevik soldier and completing intelligence missions on the Eastern Front and with the Volga Military Flotilla. Reisner became the Communist Army's first woman political commissioner. Reisner then resumed her writing, publishing her adventures of war in *The Front* (1924).

In 1921 she served as the first ambassador from Russia to Afghanistan. She died at age 32 in 1926 of typhoid fever.

Agostina, "La Saragossa"

Eighteen-year-old Agostina bravely aided in the defense of Saragossa, Spain, against French invaders in 1808. She would run into battle to rescue and nurse wounded Spanish soldiers, without caring about personal risk. Saragossa fell during the second French siege (1808–09). Afterwards La Saragossa became a national heroine and was lauded in poetry and in paintings, most notably by Goya. La Saragossa refused to accept any rewards and sought only to bear the arms of Saragossa and to maintain her military status as an engineer.

Hannah Senesh

A Hungarian-born Jew, Senesh was very outspoken about the dangers of fascism. When World War II broke out she moved to Israel and served in a commando unit dedicated to rescuing Jews from occupied territories. In 1944 she was captured in Hungary. She was killed in 1944 after suffering brutal torture.

Hannah Snell

Orphaned at 17, Hannah Snell lived for a time with her sister in London. In 1743 she married a Dutch sailor but he abandoned her soon thereafter. Snell, determined to find him, disguised herself as a man and joined a foot regiment in Coventry. Her troop traveled to Scotland to suppress the Stuart rebellion. She later told of a public flogging she sustained in Scotland for defending a girl from a sergeant's advances. The flogging caused her to desert her regiment and she became an assistant cook on a fleet bound for the East Indies. Snell took part in the fleet's attack on the French stationed at Pondicherry on the Madras Coast. To conceal her gender she treated all her wounds herself. When she returned to Europe she learned of her husband's execution and decided to end her military career. She subsequently published *The Female Soldier: or The Surprising Adventures of Hannah Snell* (1750) and received a pension for the injuries she sustained at Pondicherry. After a time she opened an inn called The Female Warrior.

Spray of Pearls

When Spray of Pearls' husband, the Sultan Al Salih Ayyúb of Egypt died in his tent in 1249, his army was left leaderless to combat the Crusaders. Spray of Pearls concealed his death, and while telling the officers that her husband's health was improving, forged her husband's signature in order to command the army. She singlehandedly led her army to victory over the powerful forces of the Crusaders while ruling over all of Egypt and hiding her husband's decaying body.

The next year, in 1250, Túrán Sháh, the sultan's elder son, traveled from Syria to become the new sultan. But the Mamluks, loyal to Spray of Pearls, killed him and proclaimed her queen of Egypt. Syria, however, would not recognize the accession of a woman. The Syrians believed that a woman was unfit to govern. Spray of Pearls was forced to marry a Mamluk of the late sultan, Aybak. Extremely unhappy, in 1257 Spray of Pearls plotted the murder of Aybak. Aybak's supporters, however, threw her from the battlements of the citadel of Cairo. Her rotting corpse lay in a ditch before it was finally buried.

Julia Stimson

A cousin of Henry L. Stimson, who served as U.S. Secretary of War and Secretary of State, Julia Stimson, born in 1881, became chief nurse of the American Red Cross in France in April 1918; later that year she was appointed director of nursing for the American Expeditionary Forces, overseeing approximately 10,000 nurses stationed throughout Europe. She went on to become acting superintendent of the Army Nurse Corps and head of the Army School of Nursing in July 1919. In July 1920 she became the first nurse to attain the relative rank of major. She later served as chairperson of the Nursing Council on National Defense (1940–42) and was promoted to colonel on the retired list in August 1948, the same year in which she died.

Miranda Stuart

Born in 1795, Miranda Stuart, alias "James Barry" had a long and distinguished career as a military doctor. The culmination of her career was being appointed Inspector-General of all British hospitals in Canada. Due to the prejudices of the time in which she lived, Stuart was forced to impersonate a man in order to practice medicine.

Orphaned at a young age, Stuart entered Edinburgh College at 16 as a frail-looking young gentleman. After receiving her medical degree, thereby becoming the first woman doctor in England, she entered military service in 1813 and was appointed staff surgeon in Canada. Throughout her career Stuart served in South Africa, the West Indies and the Crimea. During this time she performed caesarian sections, made important administrative decisions about health care, sanitation, dietary concerns and greatly helped to advance the treatment of syphilis and gonorrhea.

Trinidad Tescon

A freedom fighter in the Philippine Revolution, Tescon was born in 1848 in San Miguel de Mayuno. She enlisted in 1895 as a soldier and engaged in active fighting. Even after suffering severe injury in the battle of Saragossa, Tescon continued to fight the Spanish with unrelenting vigor.

Tescon also became the first woman to perform Red Cross work in the Philippines, organizing women to nurse injured and sick soldiers. She set up a hospital of sorts in the fort of Bick-na-Bota, where the soldiers referred to her as the "Mother of Bick-na-Bota." The International Red Cross recognized Tescon's services and when she died in 1928 she was buried in the Veteran's Tomb in Manila.

Sally Louisa Tompkins

A philanthropist, Sally Louisa Tompkins, born in 1833, converted a mansion in Richmond into a hospital at the outbreak of the U.S. Civil War. In September 1861 Confederate President Jefferson Davis ordered all private hospitals to be closed. He made an exception for Tompkins' hospital by granting her a captain's commission in the Confederate Army. The only woman with a Confederate commission, Tompkins financed and operated her Robertson Hospital until June 1865. Only 73 of the hospital's more than 1000 patients died, the lowest rate of any hospital during the war.

Katherine Towle

Born in 1898, Colonel Katherine Towle served in the Women's Reserve of the Marine Corps during World War II, becoming its director in December 1945. She continued in that post until the Women's Reserve was dissolved in June 1946. With the Women's Armed Forces Integration Act of June 12, 1948, the Women's Reserve was incorporated into the regular Marine Corps and Colonel Towle served as the first director of women.

Moscho Tzavella

A descendant of a long line of Greek guerrilla fighters and leaders, Moscho Tzavella, born in 1760, prevented Ali Pasha, the Albanian ruler of western Greece to occupy her village of Souli. Souli was the only town at that time which still resisted Turkish occupation. Tzavella organized a group of women and, armed with sticks and stones, soundly defeated the Pasha's strong army. In recognition of her accomplishment Tzavella received the title of captain and was invited to advise the village council on matters of military strategy. She died in 1803.

Loreta Velasques

After her husband, an army officer, left home to fight in the U.S. Civil War, Loreta Velasques discarded the prevailing societal restrictions on women and masqueraded as a man in order to fight for the Confederacy. With a glued-on mustache and beard, she recruited a group of soldiers and served as their commander under the name Lieutenant Harry T. Buford. She fought in several battles, including the first Battle of Bull Run and even served as a spy for a short time. Although Loreta Velasques was discovered after being wounded, she later rejoined the Confederacy as an officer in the cavalry.

Mary Edwards Walker

Mary Walker, born in 1832, graduated from Syracuse Medical College in 1855. During the U.S. Civil War she served as a nurse in the Patent Office Hospital and then as assistant surgeon in the Army of the Cumberland; she was the only woman to hold a surgeon's position during the Civil War. She continued in a variety of other posts, finally leaving the service in June 1865. She was presented with a medal of Honor shortly thereafter which she continued to wear even after an Army board revoked it in 1917 because they claimed there was no record of its award.

Women Who Aided the Military

Louisa May Alcott

American novelist Louisa May Alcott, born in Germantown, Philadelphia, in 1832, is probably best remembered for her novel *Little Women*. In 1862 Alcott worked as an Army nurse at the Union Hospital in Georgetown, Washington, D.C. Her *Hospital Sketches* (1863), based on letters she wrote home, gained her national acclaim.

Electra Apostoloy

When Electra Apostoloy, born in 1912, was 13 she became an ardent believer in communism. She therefore decided to join the Greek Communist Youth Organization (OKNE). She also organized a small number of her schoolmates into a group which provided money for exiled communists. Soon thereafter she joined the Communist Party, becoming especially involved in the role of women. She arranged classes on communism, organized strikes and served as editor of the communist journal *Youth*. Apostoloy also gave lectures in Greece and abroad on communism and the dangers of fascism. In 1935 she traveled to Paris to represent Greece at the International Conference Against Fascism.

When General Joannes Metazes became dictator, Apostoloy was imprisoned because of her beliefs from 1936 to 1938. Still she continued her classes in prison. She was then released but within a year was arrested and exiled for her pro–Communist, anti–Fascist activities. When her health declined, she was taken to a prison hospital in Athens, but escaped and lived in hiding, all the while inciting young communists to resist the Germans. She organized EPON, the core of the Greek Resistance movement. In 1944 the Greek Secret Police, supported by Germany, arrested and tortured her in order to obtain information about other leaders of the underground Communist party. Apostoloy died at the hands of her torturers without ever divulging any information.

Mary Ann Ball Bickerdyke

During the U.S. Civil War Mary Ann Bickerdyke volunteered her services to General Ulysses S. Grant, tirelessly nursing, cooking and providing supplies for Union soldiers.

Elizabeth Blackwell

The English-American doctor Elizabeth Blackwell, born in 1821, was the first woman to earn a medical degree in the United States. During the Civil War, shortly after Fort Sumter fell, Blackwell summoned a meeting of the lady managers of the infirmary to discuss the care of soldiers. Subsequently, at Cooper Union, the Women's Central Association of Relief (WCAR) was formed which also helped in the establishing of the U.S. Sanitary Commission in June 1861. During the war, Blackwell and her sister selected and trained nurses, with Elizabeth as chairman of the registration committee of the WCAR.

Belle Boyd

Belle Boyd was a Confederate spy born in 1844. She supplied the Southern armies with information on Northern troop movements. She was imprisoned and released three times by Northern troops. The third time she was caught on board a ship that was attempting to run the Union blockade. She was subsequently placed in the custody of an ensign named Sam Wylde Hardinge. They fell in love and were married but Hardinge soon died. Boyd, who would be married twice more, became an actress in England, and then a lecturer in the U.S. about her experiences. Her autobiography is entitled *Belle Boyd in Camp and Prison* (1865).

Pearl Buck

In 1938 Pearl Buck became the first American woman to be awarded the Nobel Prize for literature. When the United States entered World War II, Buck dedicated much time to the Allied effort. Involved in United China Relief she provided information for servicemen's Asian guidebooks, created radio plays for broadcast to China, publicized the war in three novels and in other propagandistic writings that won both sympathy and funds. Her essay collections such as *Of Men and Women* (1941) and *American Unity and Asia* (1942) attempted to define the war's underlying issues, predicting that white imperialist, racist, and sexist attitudes would continue to stymie world peace.

Ann Z. Caracristi

Ann Caracristi, born in 1921, worked as a cryptanalyst (i.e., code breaker) for the Army Security Agency during World War II and later became an expert in cryptanalysis of the Soviet Union and its allied countries. In 1980 she was promoted to deputy director of the National Security Agency, the highest civilian post in the organization.

Edith Cavell

After graduating as a nurse from London Hospital, Edith Cavell served as a chief of nursing at Belgium's first school for nurses at the Birkendael Medical Institute in Brussels. After the Germans invaded Brussels, the school was made into a Red Cross Hospital, where Cavell tended wounded soldiers from all countries. She also let French and British soldiers use the hospital as a hiding place before entering the Netherlands. The Germans, however, heard of Cavell's resistance work. They arrested her in August 1915 and shot her on October 12, 1915.

Julia Child

A very successful American cook, Julia Child, born in 1912, served in the Office of Strategic Services (OSS) in World War II and was stationed in Ceylon and China.

Marie Curie

A Polish-French physicist who coined the term radioactivity, Curie was the first woman to be awarded the Nobel Prize in 1903, along with her husband Pierre and colleague Henri Becquerel. (Marie and Pierre shared many joint awards for their discoveries but Pierre declined the prestigious Legion d'Honneur because it was awarded to men only.) In 1911 she became the first person to win a second Nobel Prize. During World War I she led radiation therapy services with a corps of women doctor assistants. She also earned a driving license and went to the front lines with ambulances transporting portable x-ray equipment.

Irène Joliot-Curie and Eve Curie

Irène Joliot-Curie and Eve Curie, born in 1897 and 1904, respectively, were the daughters of Pierre and Marie Curie. Irène, a Nobel Prize winner in her own right, worked as an Army nurse during World War I and was later active in the anti–Fascist movement of the 1930s. Eve became famous as an author whose biography of her mother *Madame Curie,* was translated into more than 20 languages. At the outbreak of World War II Eve coordinated women's war activities in France.

Lydia Barrington Darragh

When British officers commandeered a room at her house in Philadelphia during the American Revolution, Lydia Barrington Darragh listened through a keyhole and learned of their plans to launch a surprise attack on General George Washington. She obtained a pass out of Philadelphia and was able to send word to Washington, thus saving his army.

Deborah

An Israelite heroine, prophetess, and judge, she called the Israelites to arms, and ultimately to victory, when they were threatened by the Canaanites.

Dorothea Lynde Dix

An American nurse and social reformer who helped found 32 mental hospitals, Dorothea Lynde Dix, born in 1802, was made Chief of Nurses for the Union Army during the Civil War and in this capacity organized the Army Nursing Corps.

Eleanor of Aquitaine

Queen of England and France, mother of King Richard the Lion Heart, Eleanor of Aquitaine was born in 1122. She fought in the second crusade along with a company of 300 women.

Amalia Fleming

A Greek physician and political activist, Lady Amalia Fleming was part of the anti–Nazi underground movement during World War II. She later fought for civil rights in Greece in the 1960s and 70s. She died in 1986.

Rose O'Neal Greenhow

A Confederate spy during the U.S. Civil War, Greenhow, born in 1817, supplied information which led to the South's victory in the first Bull Run campaign.

Jeanne Laisne Hachette

When the Burgundians attempted to capture her town of Beauvais, France, in 1470, Jeanne Laisne Hachette led a group of women, armed only with hatchets, and drove the attackers away. She and her descendants were then exempt from taxation, and in her honor an annual parade was held in Beauvais, in which the women walked in front of the men.

Odette (Marie Celine) Hallowes

One of the finest British agents of World War II, Odette Hallowes worked with the French Resistance and the Special Forces in France. She once saved a colleague, Peter Churchill, from the gestapo by saying that they were married and that she had forced him to live in France.

Isabella I of Castile

Born in 1451, Isabella married Ferdinand of Aragon, thus so making them the joint rulers of all of Spain. With Ferdinand she became involved in the wars to conquer the Kingdom of Granada, which for centuries had been under Muslim domination. Following 10 years of campaigns in which Isabella took part, Granada was conquered in 1492, the same year that Christopher Columbus arrived in America on a voyage funded by the queen.

Shulamit Kishak-Cohen

Using the code name "Pearl," this mother of seven children helped smuggle many Jewish refugees into Israel while running a Lebanese spy-ring.

Mary Ludwig Hays McCauley ───────────

Mary McCauley earned the name "Molly Pitcher" during the American Revolution when she brought water and tended the wounds of the fatigued soldiers in the field. She also took over her husband's gun position when he was severely wounded during a battle at Monmouth Courthouse.

Mary Roberts Rinehart ───────────

Best-selling author Mary Roberts Rinehart was born in 1876. She worked relentlessly during World War I; she served as a European correspondent in 1915, toured camps in the United States as a representative of the secretary of war, and from Paris reported the armistice. In her novel *Bab: A Sub-Deb* (1917) a teenager who is fed up with being told that our national security is a masculine concern, uncovers an espionage ring to prove the value of women during wartime.

Rinehart served as an air raid warden in World War II. She died in 1958.

Anna Rosenberg ───────────

Owner of a public relations agency with clients such as President Franklin D. Roosevelt, General Foods and the Encyclopedia Britannica, in 1950 Anna Rosenberg was named assistant secretary of defense and helped draft programs for the Korean War and recruit women to the military.

Mary Jane Seacole ───────────

Born in Jamaica in 1805, Mary Jane Seacole received much field training in medicine, but when she offered her skills to the British during the Crimean War she was turned down because of her color. Nevertheless, Seacole journeyed to Crimea at her own expense and tended to the injured soldiers in the battlefields.

Laura Secord

A Canadian heroine of the War of 1812, when Laura Secord heard Americans were planning a surprise attack on the Canadians at Beaver Dams, she passed through American lines and walked 19 miles to warn militia commander Lieutenant James Fitzgibbon. She died in 1868 but her memory is kept alive in the name of a brand of popular Canadian chocolate.

Harriet Ross Tubman

The abolitionist Harriet Ross Tubman was born a slave in Maryland in 1821. Becoming active in the "underground railway" she helped 300 runaway slaves reach freedom in the northern states and Canada. During the Civil War she worked as a cook, laundress, nurse, scout, and spy for the Union Army. She died in 1913.

Elizabeth Van Lew

During the U.S. Civil War Elizabeth Van Lew, born in 1818, acted as a Union agent in Virginia. She visited Union prisoners in Libby Prison, supplying them with food and clothing and obtaining important military intelligence. During the year-long siege of Richmond and Petersburg (1864–1865) she gathered a great deal of information for the North and even placed a contact in the house of Jefferson Davis. She avoided suspicion of her activities by feigning mental illness. After the war, General Ulysses S. Grant personally thanked her.

Eartha Mary Magdalene White

Eartha White, social welfare, community leader, and business-woman who was better known to the poor, elderly, infirm, and homeless as the Angel of Mercy, was born in Florida in 1876. She was the offspring of a black woman and a young white man. She was soon adopted by Clara and Lafayette White, a Civil War veteran on the Union side.

During World War I Eartha White served as director of War Camp Community Services and Coordinator of Recreation in Georgia. The only woman selected to participate in the Southeast War Camp Community Service Conference she was also the only African American to attend a White House meeting of the Council of National Defense.

As World War II approached, White became an honorary colonel in the Women's National Defense Program. She established a canteen service and managed several Red Cross activities in a building she donated as a servicemen's center. Her work with A. Philip Randolph led to President Franklin Roosevelt's Executive Order 8802 prohibiting discrimination in employment in defense industries and in the federal government, and also to the instituting of the Fair Employment Practices Committee that same year.

Sarah Winnemucca

Born in Nevada, probably in 1844, Sarah Winnemucca was the daughter of Winnemucca II, Chief of the Paiute tribe. When the Bannock War started in 1878, Sarah Winnemucca volunteered to reconnoiter for the Army, for she had heard that her father and several other members of her tribe had been captured by the Bannocks.

Other scouts had refused the dangerous task but Winnemucca successfully traveled through Idaho and Oregon, freed her father and several others, and obtained important intelligence information for General G.O. Howard. Winnemucca continued to work for

General Howard as a scout, interpreter and assistant for several more years. She then campaigned to obtain better reservation lands for the Paiutes. She was promised the land many times, but government officials never kept their promise to her.

Bibliography ────────────────

Ackermann, Joan. "A Champion Who's Jumping for Joy." *Sports Il-lustrated*, Dec. 24, 1990: pp. 112–114.

Altamari, Daniela. "Women Say They Belong in Battle." *Danbury* (CT) News Times, Nov. 11, 1992. p. 15.

Bhattacharyya, S. "Belvoir Chief Bucked Long Odds." *The (Alexandria) Journal*, July 24, 1989: p. A3.

Bigelow, Julian. "UNIVAC." In *Academic American Encyclopedia*, edited by K. Anne Ranson, p. 468. vol. 19. Danbury, CT: Grolier, Inc., 1991.

Block, Maxine, ed. *Current Biography*. New York: The H.W. Wilson, Co., 1940.

_____. *Current Biography*. New York: The H.W. Wilson Co., 1942.

_____. *Current Biography*. New York: The H.W. Wilson Co., 1943.

Boatner III, Mark M. *Encyclopedia of the American Revolution*. New York: David McKay Co., Inc., 1966.

Brooks, Schoyer Polly. *Beyond the Myth: The Story of Joan of Arc*. New York: J.B. Lippincott, 1990.

Burgess, Alan. *The Lovely Sergeant*. New York: E.P. Dutton & Co., Inc., 1963.

Chase, Harold W. and Thomas Cochran, et al. *Dictionary of American History*, v. VIII. New York: Charles Scribner's Sons, 1976.

Claghorn, Charles. *Women Patriots of the American Revolution*. Me-tuchen, NJ: Scarecrow Press, Inc., 1991.

Cochran, Jacqueline. *The Stars at Noon*. Boston: Little Brown & Co., 1954.

Cornum, Rhonda, as told to Pete Copeland. *She Went to War: The Rhonda Cornum Story*. Novato, CA: Presidio Press, 1992.

Cushman, John, Jr. "Admiral Hopper's Farewell." *The New York Times*, Aug. 14, 1986.

Dever, Maria and Aileen. *Relative Origins: Famous Foster & Adopted People*. Portland, OR: National Book Co., 1992.

Family Encyclopedia of American History. New York: The Reader's Digest Association, Inc., 1975.

Faragher, John, ed. *The Encyclopedia of Colonial and Revolutionary America*. New York: Sachem Publishing Associates, Inc., 1990.

Fishwick, Marshall. *Illustrious Americans: Clara Barton*. Dallas: Silver Burdett Co., 1966.

Fleischer, Michele. "War Stories to Remember." *Glamour*. May 1991: p. 105.

_____. "We Are All Woman Warriors." *Glamour*. June, 1991: p. 152.

Frank, Allan. "Older Than UNIVAC." *Forbes*. Aug. 30, 1982: p. 141.

Fraser, Antonia. *The Warrior Queens*. New York: Alfred A. Knopft, 1989.

Fryxell, David. "Outfiguring the Navy." *American Way*. May, 1989.

Goetz, Philip W., ed. *The New Encyclopaedia Britannica*, v. 5. Chicago: Encyclopaedia Britannica, Inc., 1990.

Holm, Jeanne, Maj. Gen., USAF (Ret.). *Women in the Military: An Unfinished Revolution*. Novato, CA: Presidio Press, 1992.

Jackson, Guida N. *Women Who Ruled*. Santa Barbara, CA: ABC-CLIO, Inc., 1990.

James, Edward T., Janet Wilson James, Paul S. Boyer. *Notable American Women: A Biographical Dictionary*, vols. 1–3. Cambridge, MA: The Belknap Press of Harvard University Press, 1971.

Johnson, Allen, ed. *Dictionary of American Biography*, v. 2. New York: Charles Scribner's Sons, 1924.

Johnson, Thomas H. *The Oxford Companion to American History*. New York: Oxford University Press, 1966.

Krucoff, Carol. "Antonia Novello: A Dream Come True." *Saturday Evening Post*. June 1991: p. 38.

Lait, Matt. "First Woman to Command Fort Belvoir Retires," *The Washington Post*, Sept. 1, 1989: p. B3.

Lanker, Brian. *I Dream a World: Portraits of Black Women Who Changed America*. New York: Stewart, Tabori and Chang, 1989.

Luce-Smith, Edward A. *Joan of Arc*. New York: W.W. Norton Co., Inc., 1976.

McFadden, Robert D. "New Jersey Pilot, a Woman, Dies in Crash in Gulf." *The New York Times*. March 4, 1991: p. B2.

McGovern, Ann. *The Secret Soldier: The Story of Deborah Sampson*. New York: Four Winds Press, 1975.

McHenry, Robert, ed. *Famous American Women: A Biographical Dictionary from Colonial Times to the Present*. New York: Dover Publications, Inc., 1980.

_____. *Webster's American Military Biographies*. New York: Dover Publications, Inc., 1978.

Moritz, Charles, ed. *Current Biography*. New York: The H.W. Wilson Co., 1944.

_____. *Current Biography*. New York: The H.W. Wilson Co., 1971.

_____. *Current Biography*. New York: The H.W. Wilson Co., 1973.

Bibliography

_____. *Current Biography*. New York: The H.W. Wilson Co., 1992.

_____. *Current Biography Yearbook*. New York: The H.W. Wilson Co., 1991.

Murray, R.C. *Golden Knights: The History of the U.S. Army Parachute Team*. Canton, OH: Daring Books, 1990.

Nolan, Jeanette. *Belle Boyd: Secret Agent*. New York: Julian Messner, 1967.

Novello, Antonia, M.D. "Health Priorities for the Nineties: The Quest for Prevention." In *Vital Speeches of the Day,* edited by Tom Daly, p. 666. South Carolina: City News Publishing Co., Aug. 15, 1992.

O'Neill, Lois, ed. *The Women's Book of World Records and Achievements*. New York: Da Capo Press, Inc., 1979.

O'Toole, G.J.A. *The Encyclopedia of American Intelligence and Espionage*. New York: Facts on File, 1988.

Ottley, William. "Absolute Accolades." *Parachutist Magazine,* Dec. 1991: p. 21–22. Jason B. Bell, Ed. Alexandria, VA.

Payne, Ronald and Christopher Dobson. *Who's Who in Espionage*. New York: St. Martin's Press, 1984.

Rogan, Helen. *Mixed Company*. Boston: Beacon Press, 1981.

Rose, Mary. *Clara Barton: Soldier of Mercy*. New York: Chelsea House Publishers, 1991.

Rothe, Anna, ed. *Current Biography*. New York: The H.W. Wilson Co., 1949.

St. Lawrence, Gary. "Foote Addresses AUSA at Quarterly Assembly." *Castle,* Sept. 30, 1988: p. 3.

St. Lawrence, Gary. "Learning Belvoir; Foot by Foote." *Castle,* Jan. 18, 1989: p. 7.

Sampson, Deborah. *The Female Review: Or Memoirs of an American Young Lady*. Dedham, MA: Printed by Nathaniel and Benjamin Heaton, 1797.

Sanborn, Rick. "Thirty Years on a Fast-Moving Train." *Castle.* Sept. 1, 1989: p. 9.

Santini, Maureen. "You Did the Right Thing." *Ladies' Home Journal.* Nov. 1992.

Schroeder, Patricia. "How a Woman Would Run the Military." *New Woman.* Jan. 1993: p. 36.

Sicherman, Barbara and Carol Hurd Green. *Notable American Women: The Modern Period*. Cambridge, MA: The Belknap Press of Harvard University Press, 1980.

Smith, John. *Joan of Arc*. New York: Charles Scribner's Sons, 1973.

Smith, John J., ed. *The American Annual 1953*. New York: Americana Corporation, 1953.

Sonneborn, Liz. *Clara Barton*. New York: Chelsea House Publishers, 1992.

Spiller, Roger, ed. *Dictionary of American Military Biography,* vols. I–III. Westport, CT: Greenwood Press, 1984.

Staggenborg, Rob. "Foote Assumes Post Command." *Castle*. Oct. 7, 1988: p. 1.

Stevens, Bryna. *Deborah Sampson Goes to War*. Minneapolis: Carolrhoda Books, Inc., 1984.

Summers, Harry. *Vietnam War Almanac*. New York: Facts on File Publications, 1985.

Tinling, Marion. *Women Remembered: A Guide to Landmarks of Women's History in the U.S.* Westport, CT: Greenwood Press, 1986.

Uglow, Jennifer, ed. *The Continuum Dictionary of Women's Biography*. New York: The Continuum Publishing Co., 1982.

Valdes, Liz. "Foote Receives Honorary Doctorate." *Castle*. May 19, 1989: Ft. Belvoir, VA, p. 2.

Van Doren, Charles, ed. *Webster's American Biographies*. Springfield, MA: G & C Merriam Co., 1974.

Warner, Marina. *Joan of Arc: The Image of Female Heroism*. New York: Alfred A. Knopf, 1981.

Who Was Who in America. Chicago, IL: Marquis Who's Who Inc., 1967.

Who Was Who in America, v. 9. Wilmette, IL: MacMillan Directory, 1989.

Who Was Who in America with World Notables, v. VIII. Chicago: Marquis Who's Who Inc., 1981.

Who's Who in America 1992–93. New Jersey: Reed Publishing Inc., 1992.

Willenz, June. *Women Veterans: America's Forgotten Heroines*. New York: The Continuum Publishing Co., 1983.

Windrow, Martin and Francis K. Mason. *A Concise Dictionary of Military Biography*. London: Osprey Publishing Limited, 1975.

The World Book Encyclopedia, v. 20. Chicago, IL: Field Enterprises Educational Corporation, 1977.

Index

Index